Getting Writing Right

A HIGH SCHOOLER'S HANDBOOK ON PUNCTUATION & GRAMMAR

Getting Writing Right

A HIGH SCHOOLER'S HANDBOOK ON PUNCTUATION & GRAMMAR

Heron Books, Inc.
20950 SW Rock Creek Road
Sheridan, OR 97378

heronbooks.com

Special thanks to all the teachers and students who
provided feedback instrumental to this edition.

Third Edition © 2000, 2026 Heron Books
All Rights Reserved

ISBN: 978-0-89-739184-9

Any unauthorized copying, translation, duplication or distribution,
in whole or in part, by any means, including electronic copying, storage
or transmission, is a violation of applicable laws.

The Heron Books name and the heron bird symbol are registered
trademarks of Delphi Schools, Inc.

8 April 2026

At Heron Books, we think learning should be engaging and fun. It should be hands-on and allow students to move at their own pace.

To facilitate this, we have created learning guides that will help any student progress through this book, chapter by chapter, with confidence and interest.

Get learning guides at
heronbooks.com/learningguides.

For a final exam, email
teacherresources@heronbooks.com

We would love to hear from you!
Email us at *feedback@heronbooks.com*.

CONTENTS

Introduction 1

Part 1
PUNCTUATION

1   End Marks 5

2   The Comma (,) 9

3   The Apostrophe (') 25

4   The Colon (:) 27

5   The Semicolon (;) 29

6   Parentheses and Brackets 31

7   Quotation Marks (" ") 35

8   The Dash, Hyphen, Ellipsis, and Slash 41

9   Capitalization 47

10   Italics and Underlines 53

Part 2
GRAMMAR

11   A Comment on Grammar 57

12   Alphabetical Reference 59

APPENDIX

Grammar at a Glance 127

    Nouns 128

    Pronouns 130

    Verbs 133

    Prepositions 139

    Conjunctions 140

    Phrases 143

    Clauses 145

Index 147

INTRODUCTION

Punctuation is the use of symbols to control the flow of writing and help make the meaning clear. Grammar is how we put words together so that what we're saying or writing makes sense. This book was created for you, the high school student, to provide you with a single, go-to reference on these topics.

Part 1 covers punctuation, including capitalization. It's organized into ten simple chapters.

Part 2 covers grammar, including some usage notes. It's organized in alphabetical order so one can quickly and easily locate terms. Here you will find both definitions and examples to illustrate their meaning. Any grammar term used in the earlier part of the book can be quickly looked up in this alphabetical section if you're unsure of its meaning.

Using a no-frills approach, this book was designed to be as usable as possible. Its purpose is not to make you a grammarian or punctuation specialist. It is designed to help you become a better writer by providing a quick reference for use when writing.

With that simple introduction, we present:

Getting Writing Right
A High Schooler's Handbook
on Punctuation & Grammar

Editors

Part 1

PUNCTUATION

Chapter 1
END MARKS

You may not use the term end marks very often, but you use end marks all the time. They are the marks you use to end sentences. You learned about them in elementary school. Here are their uses.

The period

1. **A period is placed at the end of every sentence that makes a statement.**

   The ski trip was a success. Some students wanted to ski, and some chose to snowboard, but everyone had a great time.

2. **A period is used after an abbreviation.**

Co. for Company

Nov. for November

M.D. for Medical Doctor

Note: When a sentence ends in an abbreviation, an extra period is not added to end the sentence.

   While traveling overseas, I find myself eventually looking forward to returning to the U.S.

   She was listing all the shoes she needed for the summer trip: dress sandals, tennis shoes, flip-flops, etc.

3. A period is used after the numbers or letters when making a list.

List using numbers:

> To make this type of garlic bread:
> 1. Set the oven to broil.
> 2. Spread butter evenly on the sliced bread.
> 3. Add a sprinkling of garlic salt or garlic powder.
> 4. Put the slices right on the top oven rack.
> 5. Toast until lightly brown.

List using letters:

> a. Stand sideways to the tennis net.
> b. Gently throw the ball up slightly in front of you and slightly higher than you can reach with your racquet.
> c. As the ball starts dropping, reach up and strike the ball with a throwing motion while turning toward the net.

The question mark

A question mark is placed at the end of every sentence that asks a question.

> What is the weather forecast for today?
>
> You met my brother in school, didn't you?
>
> Can you believe that it is March already and it snowed yesterday?

A question mark can also be used to show doubt or uncertainty.

> Julius Caesar (born? —died 44 B.C.) was a Roman general.
>
> There's a special ingredient in your casserole. Garlic?

The exclamation point

An exclamation point goes at the end of a sentence or interjection that communicates a strong emotion such as anger, surprise, or delight. The more formal the writing, the less often it should be used.

Oh no! You just wrecked my new car!

Wow! You surprised me.

Fantastic! We have tickets to the play-off game.

Chapter 2
THE COMMA

,

Introduction

A comma is used to separate words or groups of words in a sentence. It shows that a slight pause is made when reading.

The comma has more usage rules than any other punctuation mark. In addition, there are rules that say when a comma should *not* be used.

There are different approaches to this.

One approach uses commas according to all the exact rules. Another approach uses commas as needed to make writing easy to read and understand[1]. A writer can benefit from understanding and using both approaches with judgment.

> Here the writer has used commas according to exact rules.
>
> Pressure to excel on SATs, however, causes students to begin preparing by age twelve, or even earlier, and their true education is overlooked.
>
> There is a grammar rule for each of these commas, but the sentence does not read smoothly.
>
> Here the writer has simplified the sentence and the comma use for easier reading.
>
> Pressure to excel on SATs causes students to begin preparing by age twelve or earlier, but their true education is overlooked.

---

1 An example of this view is represented in the book *How to Write Clearly: The Meaning Approach* by Ruth Beechick.

The thing to do is learn and practice the common rules, while focusing on making your writing clear. Over time, you will find yourself developing good judgment regarding comma usage.

Comma rules

1. Use a comma between items in a list or series.

A comma is placed between words, phrases, or clauses in a list or series and before the *and* or *or* preceding the last item in the list.

> Before the start of school, I bought a new computer, pencils, pens, and highlighters. (words in a list)

> We searched for that recipe in the kitchen, in the pantry, and even in the dining room. (phrases in a series)

> The parents decided they would let their teenage children decide what they would wear, what they would eat, and when they would do their chores each day. (clauses in a series)

> Before leaving for vacation, I washed the breakfast dishes, father loaded the car and closed the garage door, and mother locked both doors to the house. (clauses in a series)

Note: Some writers leave out the final comma in a series. This can be done if the meaning of the sentence remains clear. If the meaning would be unclear without the comma, use it.

> This semester I plan to take classes in French literature, chemistry, advanced algebra, plants, and animal biology.

In this sentence, placing the final comma makes it clear that *plant biology* and *animal biology* are separate classes. Without the final comma, a reader might think that the student is taking one biology class on plants and animals.

2. Use commas when writing an exact quotation.

A comma is used to separate a quotation from expressions such as "he said" or "she exclaimed," whether the expression comes before, after, or in the middle of the quotation.

"I can't go out tonight," Hannah said sadly, "because I have to prepare my presentation for tomorrow."

Sally replied, "That's all right. I should study anyway."

"It was the best of times, it was the worst of times," wrote Dickens.

3. Use commas around a person or thing being addressed.

The name of a person or thing being addressed in a sentence is enclosed by commas.

I'm happy to tell you, *George*, that your work has been excellent.

My friends, it is good to see you again.

You shine, *my lovely lamp*, as a beacon in the darkness.

Please don't interrupt me, *Mary*.

4. Use a comma between multiple modifiers.

When multiple adjectives modify the same noun, use a comma between them.

Our *old, red* barn could stable twenty horses and cows.
Old and *red* both modify the barn. The comma is a substitute for *and*.

It was a short, intriguing, and animated presentation.
All three adjectives modify *presentation*.

When the last adjective must be next to the noun for it to make sense, don't put a comma between it and the noun.

> We watched their outstanding *basketball team.*
>
> He cleared all the trash from the filthy, rundown *cow barn.*

The test is whether you can change the order of the modifying words and replace the commas with *and*. If you can, the comma belongs. If you can't, don't use a comma.

> We watched their *basketball and outstanding* team.
> It doesn't make any sense. Thus, there are no commas.
>
> He cleared all the trash from the *rundown and filthy* cow barn.
> It does make sense. Thus, a comma between *filthy* and *rundown*.
>
> He cleared all the trash from the *cow and rundown and filthy* barn.
> It doesn't make sense. The word *cow* needs to be next to the word *barn*, so there's no comma between *rundown* and *cow*.

In some cases, the first adjective is actually modifying the second adjective, not the noun. Don't separate these with a comma.

> She found *pale purple* flowers in the woods.
> *Pale* modifies *purple* not *flowers*, so no comma is needed.
>
> Again notice that you can't reverse the order and add *and* without changing the meaning: *purple and pale flowers* means something different than *pale purple flowers.*

When an adjective or adverb is repeated for emphasis, use a comma between them.

> The house was *very, very* old and needed extensive repairs.
>
> We spoke to *many, many* people during the conference.

5. Use commas to write dates and locations.

In dates written in month-day-year sequence, use a comma after the day and the year.

Incorrect: The colonies declared their independence on July 2, *1776* at Independence Hall.

Correct: The colonies declared their independence on July 2, *1776*, at Independence Hall.

When the only elements of a date are the month and year, no comma is needed.

Incorrect: The Lunar New Year was celebrated in a different way in February, 2017.

Correct: The Lunar New Year was celebrated in a different way in February 2017.

When locations that have more than one term are in a sentence, put a comma after each part, such as city and state or province and country.

Incorrect: I lived in *Boston, Massachusetts* for 10 years.

Correct: I lived in *Boston, Massachusetts*, for 10 years.

Incorrect: *Alberta, Canada* was to be the location of his next project.

Correct: *Alberta, Canada,* was to be the location of his next project.

6. Use a comma after an introductory adverb clause.

It is generally accepted to use a comma after an introductory **adverb clause.** When an adverb clause comes at the end of a sentence, however, a comma (and the slight pause it indicates) is not usually needed.

Introductory adverb clause

Because I must be back by noon, I'm leaving early.

Ever since she learned to drive a car, she hasn't ridden her bicycle.

Because it had been rainy all month, my family decided to vacation down south.

After they had cut down the trees, they began to pull up the stumps.

Although Abdul had never seen her before, he recognized her at once.

As if he had been riding horses all his life, Javier swung into the saddle.

Adverb clause at the end

I'm leaving early *because I must be back before noon.*

She hasn't ridden her bicycle *since she learned to drive a car.*

Javier swung into the saddle *as if he'd been riding horses all his life.*

7. Use a comma after an introductory participle phrase.

It is generally accepted to use a comma after an introductory participle phrase.

A writer may use some judgment on this rule, however. Sometimes a comma is vital to make the meaning clear.

Unclear: *Baking carefully* the cook worked slowly.

Clear: *Baking carefully,* the cook worked slowly.

Without the comma, the first sentence could be saying the cook was being baked carefully!

Other times, using a comma is unnecessary and makes the sentence choppy, especially in a short sentence.

Swimming fastest he won the race.

Bored beyond description we decided to go for a walk.

As always, use commas to create sentences that read smoothly and clearly.

Blackened and twisted by a bolt of lightning, the old tree continued to live.

Deprived of its prey, the cheetah slunk back into the tall grass.

Unknown to most people, the octopus is an intelligent animal.

He won the race at last, and *waving to his fans,* he began the victory lap.

8. Use a comma after a long introductory prepositional phrase that modifies.

A long introductory prepositional phrase, or a series of two or more prepositional phrases that modify a sentence, is usually followed by a comma.

After the long and drawn out night, the campers were happy to see the dawn.

By a sunny clearing in the deepest part of the forest, Snow White found the house of the Seven Dwarfs.

As a writer, you must judge when an introductory phrase is long enough to want the reader to pause while reading the sentence. If a comma is not used, the reader will not pause. By reading the sentence aloud, it usually becomes clear if a comma is needed.

Reads smoothly without a comma: *After dark* we couldn't see a thing when we went out.

Comma needed for a pause in reading: *With twinkling stars in her deep blue eyes and an undying love for adventure in her youthful heart,* the young woman set out for the mountains of Central Asia to write a new chapter in her life's story.

9. Using a comma is optional after a short introductory modifier.

Commas are optional after short introductory modifiers that consist of single words or short phrases, depending on whether you feel a slight pause is needed or helpful. Either way is correct.

Correct: *Unfortunately* no one was home.

Also correct: *Unfortunately,* no one was home.

Correct: *In 1963* the Supreme Court struck down prayer in schools.

Also correct: *In 1963,* the Supreme Court struck down prayer in schools.

Correct: *Despite everything* the team won.

Also correct: *Despite everything,* the team won.

10. Do not use a comma after most introductory conjunctions and adverbs.

a. Sometimes a sentence starts with a conjunction, which joins it with the previous sentence. Because a conjunction joins things and a comma separates things, it's confusing to start a sentence with a conjunction and follow it with a comma.

Incorrect: *But,* they were late for breakfast.

Correct: *But* they were late for breakfast.

Incorrect: *So,* I decided to send Jackie.

Correct: *So* I decided to send Jackie.

b. In modern writing, this rule usually applies to single introductory adverbs to improve the flow of the sentence.

Older usage: *Then,* the ground opened and swallowed them.

Modern usage: *Then* the ground opened and swallowed them.

Older usage: *Soon,* the cavalry arrived.

Modern usage: *Soon* the cavalry arrived.

Then and *soon* move the action along. They are not sentence interrupters, and they do not require any pause.

11. Use a comma between independent clauses.

It is a long-accepted rule to use a comma after the first independent clause of a compound sentence and before the conjunction (*for, and, nor, but, or, yet* and *so*).

This rule is not always used in modern writing, but using it makes long sentences easier to read.

> Henry remembered to pick up the birthday card, and he also bought a gift.
>
> She became aware that she was walking home, yet she had no recollection of the previous four hours.
>
> I started work early this morning, but I still did not get all my work done.
>
> Betty got here yesterday, so she had first choice of the reserved rooms.

If the first clause of a compound sentence is very short, the comma is optional.

> Accepted: I took a shower and I ate breakfast early.
>
> Also accepted: I took a shower, and I ate breakfast early.
>
> Accepted: I was late so I had to work hard to catch up.
>
> Also accepted: I was late, so I had to work hard to catch up.

Note: If two verbs share a subject, there is only one independent clause, so no comma is used before the conjunction.

> Incorrect: Visitors must knock on the door, *or* ring the bell when they come.
>
> Correct: Visitors must knock on the door *or* ring the bell when they come.
>
> The verbs *knock* and *ring* share the subject *visitors*.

Incorrect: The children played outdoors all afternoon, *and* had a wonderful time.

Correct: The children played outdoors all afternoon *and* had a wonderful time.

The two verbs *played* and *had* share the subject *children*.

12. Use a comma with a nonrestrictive clause or phrase.

A nonrestrictive (or nonessential) clause or phrase is one that modifies or renames or comments on something in the sentence, but isn't necessary for the sentence to make sense. Nonrestrictive clauses or phrases are set off by commas.

Before moving to South Africa, Art Tillman was born in London.

The prepositional phrase *Before moving to South Africa* is nonrestrictive because the sentence would make sense without it.

I am planning a trip to Shanghai, *since it is my favorite city in China.*

The clause *since it is my favorite city in China* is nonrestrictive because the sentence is still a logical sentence and understandable without it.

Lying over there by the fire, my poodle is over ten years old.

The nonrestrictive participle phrase modifies *poodle* by giving more information about it but is not essential to identifying the particular poodle.

Compare the above example to this:

I have two gray poodles, but the one lying by the fire is older.

The restrictive phrase *lying by the fire* identifies a particular dog, so no comma encloses the phrase.

Dressed with rings on her fingers and bells on her toes, Fatima performed the Dance of the Seven Veils.

A comma follows the nonrestrictive participle phrase because it modifies *Fatima* but doesn't add anything essential in identifying her. The sentence still makes sense without it.

Jim had helped to recover the pirates' treasure, *which was worth a fortune.*

The nonrestrictive clause is set off with a comma because it modifies *treasure* by telling more about it but is not essential for a logical sentence.

13. Use a comma at both ends of a nonrestrictive element in mid-sentence.

Two commas, one at each end, enclose a nonrestrictive (nonessential) element in mid-sentence. This rule applies to a single word, phrase, or clause.

A common nonrestrictive element is the sentence interrupter, which is a word or phrase added to show emotion or emphasize something that isn't vital to the meaning of the sentence.

Perry's wife of twenty years, *surprisingly*, spoke only Hindi.

I fumbled in the dark with my keys and, *as usual*, came up with the wrong one.

My father, *as you may know*, won prizes for his rhododendrons.

Commas also enclose another type of nonrestrictive element, the noun restatement.

Her twin sister, *Tammy*, is living in Prague now.

Juan Pablo's thoroughbred, *The Pride of Puebla*, won the last race of the season.

General Eisenhower, *who was later elected President of the U.S.*, commanded the Allied forces during the Normandy invasion.

The nonrestrictive clause is set off with commas because it renames *General Eisenhower* by giving more information about him, but it is not necessary to the basic idea of the sentence.

14. Do not use a comma with a restrictive phrase or clause.

A restrictive (or essential) clause or phrase is one that is essential to the sentence for it to be logical and clear, usually by identifying something. These are not set off with commas.

I have two gray poodles, but the one lying by the fire is older.

The restrictive phrase *lying by the fire* identifies a particular dog, so no comma encloses the phrase.

Compare the above example to this:

Lying over there by the fire, my poodle is over ten years old.

The nonrestrictive phrase modifies *poodle* by giving more information about it but is not essential to identifying the particular poodle.

That duck *swimming in the pond* belongs to my son.

The restrictive phrase *swimming in the pond* both modifies and identifies a particular duck.

This is the box *that I found in the attic.*

The restrictive clause *that I found in the attic* identifies a particular box.

Al is the man *whose hat I found.*

The restrictive clause *whose hat I found* identifies a particular man.

People *who were sitting in the back of the room* couldn't hear the speaker.

The restrictive clause *who were sitting in the back of the room* identifies the specific people being referred to.

15. Do not place a comma between a subject and its verb.

Do not separate a subject and verb in a sentence or clause by a comma. This error is commonly made when a subject is composed of many words.

Incorrect: *The person you should really be speaking with,* is out to lunch right now.

Correct: *The person you should really be speaking with* is out to lunch right now.

Incorrect: *What you don't understand,* is that I've heard all this before.

Correct: *What you don't understand* is that I've heard all this before.

Incorrect: *The mule, the horse, and the cow,* must all be sold as soon as possible.

Correct: *The mule, the horse, and the cow* must all be sold as soon as possible.

Within the subject there is a comma because it is a series of three items. All three items make up the subject.

Correct: *The many times the dentist told you to brush your teeth regularly* seems to have made a good impression on you.

The long subject isn't followed by a comma.

Also correct: *The many times the dentist told you to brush your teeth regularly, Benny,* seems to have made a good impression on you.

The long subject is followed by the name of the person being addressed. That is the reason for the comma per comma rule 3.

16. Do not place a comma between a verb and direct object, or between a preposition and its object.

A pause is not needed so a comma isn't placed between a verb and direct object, or between a preposition and the object of the preposition.

Incorrect: I gave him, *twenty reasons, and a direct order* not to buy the property too soon.

Correct: I gave him *twenty reasons and a direct order* not to buy the property too soon.

Incorrect: The king made him a present of, *four golden chairs, and a mahogany table.*

Correct: The king made him a present of *four golden chairs and a mahogany table.*

17. Do not use a comma between items connected by *and* or *or*.

Do not insert commas between two or more items that are connected by the conjunctions *and* or *or*.

Incorrect: A Boy Scout needs a pocketknife, *and* a compass, *and* some matches.

Correct: A Boy Scout needs a pocketknife *and* a compass *and* some matches.

This is a list of three items; because each item is connected by *and*, no commas are needed.

Incorrect: Her uncle gave her an expensive watch, *and* a new car.

Correct: Her uncle gave her an expensive watch *and* a new car.

Incorrect: I am expecting either the Prince of Bulgaria, *or* his brother.

Correct: I am expecting either the Prince of Bulgaria *or* his brother.

18. Use a comma for clarity.

Use a comma wherever needed to make your meaning clear or to keep the reader from being confused.

Unclear: The rebels fired cannonballs and mortar shells and an explosion rocked the fort.

Clear: The rebels fired cannonballs and mortar shells, and an explosion rocked the fort.

Without the comma, the reader might start to think that an explosion is a third thing that the rebels fired.

Unclear: Sam dropped his rifle and a rabbit leaped out of the brush.

Clear: Sam dropped his rifle, and a rabbit leaped out of the brush.

Without the comma, the reader's first impression may be that the hunter dropped both his rifle and a rabbit. The comma signals the reader to switch gears.

Unclear: I had told her so she wasn't surprised when he called.

Clear: I had told her, so she wasn't surprised when he called.

In this sentence, *so* can have three possible meanings. Without the comma the reader cannot predict which of the meanings of *so* is intended without reading the rest of the sentence.

Where another comma rule seems to conflict with this one, decide what to do based on what will make it clearest to the reader.

19. Do not use a comma without a specific rule.

If you find yourself putting commas in places they do not belong, make this last comma rule your first comma rule.

Chapter 3
THE APOSTROPHE

'

The use of the apostrophe has changed over the last four hundred years. The first rule given reflects the original use.

1. **An apostrophe is used to show where letters have been left out or changed in a contraction.**

    She did not swim yesterday. She *didn't* swim yesterday.

    Clara has not been here. Clara *hasn't* been here.

    He will not be able to attend the meeting. He *won't* be able to attend the meeting.

2. **An apostrophe shows the possessive case of nouns.**

    The *child's* puzzle was surprisingly difficult.

    That *bakery's* cookies are spicy and sweet.

    The *boys'* dormitory passed inspection.

You will occasionally find the s omitted when it is a name ending in an *s* or *z* sound, though both are accepted.

| Thomas's class | or | Thomas' class |
| Roz's house | or | Roz' house |

To form the possessive for a plural noun that doesn't end in s, add an apostrophe and an s.

> the children's hour
>
> the oxen's feed
>
> the geese's nests

To form the possessive for a plural noun ending in s, simply add an apostrophe at the end.

> the employees' parking lot

Apostrophes are not used to show the possessive case of personal pronouns.

> Incorrect: These cookies are mine. I didn't take *your's*.
>
> Correct: These cookies are mine. I didn't take *yours*.

Note: When a personal pronoun is used as an adjective showing possession, the same rule applies: Apostrophes are not used.

> Incorrect: Give the dog *it's* food. (*It's* means *it is*.)
>
> Correct: Give the dog *its* food. (*Its* means *belonging to it*.)

Apostrophes are not used to form the plurals of nouns. (The only exception to this is covered in the next rule.)

> Incorrect: The *cat's* slept under the house.
>
> Correct: The *cats* slept under the house.

3. **An apostrophe plus s is used to form plurals of letters or numerals.**

> There are five *A's* in that sentence.
>
> The teacher had them write a row of *6's*.

Chapter 4
THE COLON

Generally, a colon means "note what follows."

Here are common uses for a colon.

1. **A colon is used after a complete statement that is followed by a list.**

   Take everything you'll need for camping: tent, sleeping bag, soap, toothbrush, cooking utensils and food.

   Take everything you'll need for camping:
   - tent
   - sleeping bag
   - soap
   - toothbrush
   - cooking utensils
   - food

2. **A colon may be used after a complete statement when it is followed by one that essentially restates the same idea. The restatement may be in different words that add to the prior statement.**

   Don't bother to clean up the work site: just leave your tools and materials where they are.

Napoleon was finally defeated in 1815: his army laid down their weapons for the last time at the Battle of Waterloo.

3. A colon is used before a quotation only when it is formally introduced.

Remember what Horace Greeley said: "Go West, young man!"

The editor of the dictionary stated his foremost purpose when he said: "This dictionary is intended to clarify the meanings of words in the simplest manner possible."

Incorrect: Mateo said to his team: "Play your best game and we'll win."

Correct: Mateo said to his team, "Play your best game and we'll win."

This is simply a quotation, not one that is formally introduced.

4. A colon is used after the salutation of a business letter.

Dear Sir:

Dear Madam:

Dear Ms. Smith:

5. When writing the time, a colon is used between the numerals indicating the hours and minutes. When seconds are included, another colon precedes the seconds.

12:20 A.M.

8:30 P.M.

Her race-winning time for the marathon was 2:35:12.

She completed the race in 2 hours, 35 minutes and 12 seconds.

Chapter 5
THE SEMICOLON

A semicolon indicates a greater pause than a comma, but less than the full stop of a period.

1. Use semicolons to join two complete thoughts with or without a transition.

Semicolons can be used to join related, complete thoughts (independent clauses).

My father was a baker; I expect I'll be a baker too.

The teacher quickly checked the test for correct answers; they were all correct.

Today is only Wednesday; *nevertheless*, we have a lot of catching up to do before the weekend.

Ilsa dances beautifully; *on the other hand*, her singing needs work.

I love hot dogs; *however*, I won't eat the hot dogs they serve at Benny's restaurant.

A semicolon should not be followed by a sentence fragment.

Incorrect: There goes Judy; the brightest girl in the class.

Correct: There goes Judy; she is the brightest girl in the class.

Correct: There goes Judy, the brightest girl in the class.

2. **Use a semicolon to show a cause-effect relationship between two independent clauses.**

It's late; I guess I'll be going to bed.

The first clause, *It's late*, expresses the cause of the second clause, *I'll be going to bed*.

Jasper woke up with a stomachache; it must have been something he ate.

Here, the second clause expresses the cause of the first clause.

3. **Use a semicolon to contrast two statements**

My friend Fred is very tall; his sister is tiny.

Those were the last of the dark days; a new light was about to dawn.

Chapter 6
PARENTHESES AND BRACKETS

Parentheses

Parentheses are used in pairs to set off additional information within a sentence, paragraph or other text. A word, phrase or sentence can be placed within parentheses to comment, explain or amplify some text. (The word *parentheses* is plural for the word *parenthesis*. Because they are usually used in pairs, the word *parenthesis* is less often used, so may be less familiar to you.)

Such information may include the following:

1. **A comment not vital to the meaning of the sentence.**

   Terry (from Seattle) went to cooking school in France.

   Prince William of England (second in line to become king) attended the charity event in London.

   If the additional information is addressing someone or is a noun restatement, commas should be used to set it off, not parentheses.

   I'm not sure I understand, Kristi, why you want to go tomorrow.

   Terry, my youngest sister, went to cooking school in France.

2. **References and page numbers in documentation.**

   A résumé for a recent graduate should include the most important educational accomplishments (*Careers Oregon 2016*, 15).

   Careers Oregon 2016 includes a career guide for health services (pp. 43-45).

3. **Dates, such as for birth, death or publication.**

George Orwell (1903-1950) completed his final novel, *Nineteen Eighty-Four*, shortly before his death.

The National Aeronautics and Space Administration (founded October 1, 1958) has launched several deep-space probes.

Use of Punctuation with Parentheses

There are several rules for the handling of parentheses with other punctuation marks.

1. **When the words in parentheses come at the end of the sentence, the period (or other end mark) is placed outside the parentheses.**

    The frog jumped into the pond (the large one out back).

    I told her I understood her perfectly (when I didn't).

    What did he just say (in that last sentence)?

2. **When the statement in parentheses is a complete sentence that makes sense by itself, it is written as a complete sentence with a capital at the beginning and the end mark placed within the parentheses.**

    The frog jumped into the pond. (As a tadpole, it had started life in that pond.)

    I told her I understood her perfectly. (Did you understand what she said?)

3. **When a parenthetical sentence comes in the middle of another sentence, it is not normally written as a complete sentence with a capital at the beginning and an end mark within the parentheses.**

Incorrect: Old Charles Spencer (He is a horse veterinarian.) attended the town meeting.

Correct: Old Charles Spencer (he is a horse veterinarian) attended the town meeting.

Acceptable, but best avoided: Old Charles spencer (Did you know he is a horse veterinarian?) attended the town meeting.

A partial exception to this rule concerns question marks and exclamation points, which can be used in parenthetical phrases within sentences.

Suzan quit the team (can you believe it?) even after the coach's inspirational talk.

We hope to make over $50,000 profit (that's right, $50,000!) in the next month.

4. **Commas (or other punctuation marks) are not placed before parentheses.**

Incorrect: After finding the mysterious lake, (its depth unknown) the children explored it all summer.

Correct: After finding the mysterious lake (its depth unknown), the children explored it all summer.

Incorrect: Was she the one who called that night? (the night it all started).

Correct: Was she the one who called that night (the night it all started)?

Brackets [ ]

Brackets are similar to parentheses but have their own specific uses.

1. **Brackets are used to insert something into text that is already in parentheses.**

   The pilot flew to Florida (where Jerry [Bill's uncle] had been trained) for further flight training.

2. **Brackets are used to correct an error, make a slight change, or insert some additional data into a quotation.**

   "[O]ur fathers brought forth upon this continent a new nation, . . ."
   (The "O" isn't capitalized in the original because it wasn't the beginning of the sentence.)

   "Because of the nail the [horse]shoe was lost."

   "In the year 1717 we spied a tiny, wooded island [probably Johnson Island] off the starboard bow."
   (The idea that it might be Johnson Island is inserted by a later writer.)

3. **Brackets are used to communicate acting or stage directions in a play.**

   Jennifer: [running off stage] I am late for my meeting!

Chapter 7
QUOTATION MARKS

" "

Quotation marks are always used in pairs. The first of the pair (") is usually called the "opening" quotation mark and the second of the pair (") the "closing" quotation mark.

1. Use quotation marks to show direct quotations in dialogue.

A direct quotation is the exact words in the same order that a speaker or writer used them. Quotation marks are used to enclose a direct quotation. Quotation marks are not used for an indirect quotation, where the exact words of a speaker or writer are not being used.

> **Direct quotation:** The manager said, "You'll be promoted next month."
>
> **Indirect quotation:** The manager told her she was going to be promoted next month.
>
> **Direct quotation:** "Where should we go for vacation?" she asked.
>
> **Indirect quotation:** She asked where we should go for vacation.
>
> **Direct quotation:** The candidate was quoted as saying, "We must all find a new way of viewing the welfare system. The current system is doomed to fail utterly over the next decade."
>
> **Direct quotation:** The candidate said that we must find a "new way of viewing the welfare system." He feels the way the system is run right now it "is doomed to fail utterly."
>
> **Indirect quotation:** The candidate spoke about the need to change the way we look at the welfare system, asserting that it will fail within the next ten years.

Dialogue Format

Every time the speaker changes in a dialogue with direct quotations, a new paragraph should be started. This makes it easy for the reader to see who is saying what.

Incorrect:

"What did you find?" Oliver asked. "I'm not sure," Sarah replied, "but it certainly is a mystery." "Where is it, Sarah?" "It's in the front room of the abandoned house next door," she said. "It may be a huge book or a small chest but I'm trying to decipher the symbols on it before I open it."

Correct:

"What did you find?" Oliver asked.

"I'm not sure," Sarah replied, "but it certainly is a mystery."

"Where is it, Sarah?"

"It's in the front room of the abandoned house next door," she said. "It may be a huge book or a small chest but I'm trying to decipher the symbols on it before I open it."

Use of Punctuation with Quotation Marks

When a statement in quotation marks in a dialogue is followed by a phrase telling who said it, a comma (not a period) is placed at the end.

"My cat is up in that tree," the little boy said.

"I have a letter for you," she said.

If the line of dialogue is a question or exclamation, a question mark or exclamation point (no comma) is placed at the end of the line before the closing quotation mark.

"Who wants pizza and salad for lunch?" Mother asked.

"There goes my cat!" Goldie shrieked.

When a clause such as *He asked* or *Sierra said* introduces the line of dialogue, it is followed by a comma and the end of the line receives its usual punctuation.

> He asked, "Why are there so many people here?"
>
> She said, "I'm glad we decided to come."
>
> Jason cheered, "Our team won!"

When there is no "he said/she said" type of phrase, there is no need for a comma, providing the sentence is clear.

> I agreed with John's point that "nobody should ask her about it."
>
> When you were saying how "all Allan's friends are so much taller than he is," I had to laugh.

2. **When quoting more than one sentence in a paragraph, place the closing quotation mark at the end of the last sentence in the paragraph, not after each sentence.**

> Sarah explained, "The strange object is in the front room of the abandoned house next door. It may be a huge book or a small chest. I'm not sure but I want to decipher the symbols on it before I open it."
>
> "All musical instruments have their own histories, from the most primitive forms to the latest advanced versions. But the story of the development of the keyboard instruments is probably the most fascinating of all." (Berger, *The Science of Music*, 67)

Similarly, when quoting more than one paragraph, place the closing quotation mark at the end of the last paragraph being quoted, not at the end of each paragraph.

> Here are the results of the experiment:
>
> "The iron nail placed in water for three days began to oxidize. Reddish rust, iron oxide, formed all along the nail.

"The copper penny placed in water for three days did not change in appearance. When vinegar and salt were added to the solution, a blue-green copper oxide compound appeared on the penny."

3. **Single quotation marks are used when quoted words are in text that is already in quotation marks.**

The professor said, "I'd like to discuss your recent reading, including O'Henry's 'The Gift of the Magi' and the article, 'Integrity in the Justice System,' before you do your assignment."

Our teacher told the class, "Many of you are misusing the phrase 'beat around the bush.'"

4. **Quotation marks can be used to enclose the titles of short stories, songs, poems, articles from magazines or newspapers, and book chapters.**

Short story: "The Last of the Troubadours" from *The O'Henry Short Story Collection*

Song: "Blackbird" by Paul McCartney

Poem: "After Apple-Picking" by Robert Frost

Article: "A Woman's Place Is in Cyberspace" from *Fast Company* magazine

Book chapter title: "An Unexpected Party" from *The Hobbit*

When quotation marks are used in text, commas and periods are placed inside closing quotation marks; colons and semicolons are placed outside closing quotation marks.

When she submitted her poem, "The Rainbow Path," it won an award.

The judges liked the imagery used in "The Rainbow Path."

The author used the following images in "The Rainbow Path": clear skies, stormy skies, soaring birds, sheltering birds.

Most of the class loved "The Rainbow Path"; however, I was not one of them.

5. **If using slang, unusual expressions, or technical terms, enclose them in quotation marks.**

That coffee, believe it or not, costs a "fiver."

Maybe she knows how to snowboard, but she sure is "goofy footed" when she comes down the slope.

It's the "polarity" that changes, not the quality of being magnetic.

Chapter 8
THE DASH, HYPHEN, ELLIPSIS, AND SLASH

The dash —

A dash (—) is longer than a hyphen (-). Most word processing programs automatically create a dash if you type two hyphens together. There is no space before or after a dash.

A dash is generally used in a sentence to create a break in thought, similar to a comma but stronger. It's best used sparingly.

1. Use a dash to set off a summarizing statement after a series.

In this case, a dash is used instead of a colon and it makes the writing less formal.

> I admired Christine, Janice, Ellen, and Claire—all sisters who became musicians.
>
> We sent letters, calls, and emails to our U.S. Senators—none were effective in preventing passage of that law.

2. Use a dash to show an interruption or sudden change of thought.

A dash can be used to indicate an interruption in the flow of writing or a sudden change of thought.

> Once we reached the top of the ridge—and it had been no easy task to get there—we saw that we were still a long way from the peak.

Many American colonists did support the British government—despite the hardships caused by taxation.

3. Use a dash to set off a noun restatement that contains a comma.

The Constitution of the United States—the one I studied in depth in grad school, and the one I have become so passionate about—grants to every citizen equal justice before the law.

The hyphen

A hyphen is used to join words, parts of words or numbers. It is typed without spaces before or after it.

1. Use a hyphen when splitting a word at the end of a line.

Since most writing is now done with word processing programs, words that are too long to fit on a line are usually moved to the next line rather than hyphenated. If it is necessary to hyphenate a word at the end of the line, it should only be done at a normal syllable break. A dictionary will show the syllable breaks in a word. If a normal syllable break might leave a single hyphenated letter separated from the rest of the word, it shouldn't be left at the beginning or end of a line.

Incorrect: After years of telling her story to groups of five hundred to a thousand executives at a time, she decided to *publ-ish* her memoirs.

Correct: After years of telling her story to groups of five hundred to a thousand executives at a time, she decided to *pub-lish* her memoirs.

Incorrect: Once she'd had a few ski lessons, she went out *a-gain* every weekend that winter.

Correct: Once she'd had a few ski lessons, she went out *again* every weekend that winter.

2. **Use a hyphen in compound modifiers that come before the noun.**

When two or more modifiers act together as an adjective, they can be joined with a hyphen. This is done to clarify that both modifiers together describe the noun that follows them. Otherwise, the first modifier might seem to modify the second one.

> I live on a *dead-end* street.
>
> When he started this job, he was a *fresh-faced* kid.
>
> It was a *never-to-be-forgotten* day.
>
> They have a *three-year-old* son.
>
> She skied all day under a *steel-blue* sky.

3. **Don't use a hyphen when a compound modifier comes after the noun, or the first modifier is an adverb ending in -ly.**

A compound modifier is not hyphenated when it follows the noun it is modifying.

There are exceptions. When in doubt, check a dictionary.

> That day was *never to be forgotten.*
>
> Their son is *three years old.*
>
> She skied all day under a sky of *steel blue.*

Also, a compound modifier is not hyphenated if the first modifier is an adverb ending in *-ly* because the adverb is modifying the adjective, not the noun.

> an *extraordinarily* intelligent man
>
> a *vastly* important scheme
>
> a *quickly* fading sunset

4. Use a hyphen to write certain prefixes.

When using *ex-* meaning former, *self-* and *all-* as prefixes, a hyphen should be used.

    John's *ex-wife* normally drove his children to school.

    The *ex-mayor* continued to manage several community activities.

    There are no *self-serve* gas stations in Oregon.

    The girl was so *self-absorbed* she didn't notice that anyone else had problems.

    As a child, I believed my mother was *all-knowing* and *all-powerful*.

5. Use a hyphen to write out numbers.

When writing numbers in text, always hyphenate the numbers *twenty-one* through *ninety-nine* (21 through 99), whether or not they make up part of a larger number.

    There were *twenty-six* students in the class.

    She earned *one hundred seventy-five* dollars this afternoon.

    Five thousand three hundred forty-two people live in my town.

Hyphenate compound modifiers containing numbers, including fractions used as compound modifiers.

    To train, we did a *six-mile* run every day.

    She adopted a *three-month-old* puppy.

    The company had a *one-third* increase in production last year.

The ellipsis •••

An ellipsis is used to show where a word or words have been omitted from quoted material in a piece of writing. Its use implies the basic meaning of the quote hasn't been changed by the omission.

> **Original quote:** "Four score and seven years ago our fathers brought forth on this continent, a new nation, conceived in Liberty, and dedicated to the proposition that all men are created equal."
>
> **Quote with omissions:** "Four score and seven years ago our fathers brought forth . . . a new nation, . . . dedicated to the proposition that all men are created equal."
>
> (*Gettysburg Address,* Abraham Lincoln)

When the end of the quoted sentence or when one or more entire sentences are omitted, four dots are used—a three-dot ellipsis and a normal period:

> "As a clerk he proved honest and efficient. . . . A man who begins by strict honesty in his youth is not likely to change as he grows older. . . ."
>
> ("Honest Abe," by Horatio Alger)

The slash

The slash is also called a forward slash or, if you want to be fancy, a virgule.

1. A slash is most commonly used to mean *or*.

This is usually used in informal writing with no spaces typed before or after the slash.

> Your girlfriend/boyfriend is welcome at the event.
>
> Would you like pizza/tacos for dinner?
>
> Freshman should bring blankets and/or quilts for their dorm room.

2. A slash can be used to form abbreviations in informal writing.

This is only used in informal writing with no spaces typed before or after the slash.

Send the package c/o (care of) my mother.

Serve this dish w/o (without) onions.

In hot climates, a/c (air conditioning) is vital to stay comfortable in the summer.

3. A slash is used to write dates and fractions.

3/16/17 or 3/16/2017 (March 16, 2017)

7/4/1776 (July 4, 1776)

3/4

13/100

4. A slash can be used to show a line break in a poem, song or play.

In this use, no space is typed before the slash and one space is typed after it.

"Jingle Bells/ Jingle Bells/ Jingle all the way."

(James Lord Pierpont)

"The quality of mercy is not strained/ It droppeth as the gentle rain from heaven/ Upon the place beneath. It is twice blest/ It blesseth him that gives and him that takes. . . ."

(from *Merchant of Venice*, William Shakespeare)

Chapter 9
CAPITALIZATION

The rules of capitalization given here are the most common. There are additional rules that can be found in grammar references for professional writers.

1. **Capitalize the first word in a sentence.**

    She ran around the track eight times.

    Do you plan to complete your project this month?

2. **Capitalize the first word of a direct quotation.**

    He said, "You have to train for years to be prepared to compete at the Olympics."

    She said, "We can leave for Europe next week."

    "Appreciation is a wonderful thing. It makes what is excellent in others belong to us as well."
    –Voltaire

    Exception: Don't capitalize the first word of a quotation when it is part of your own sentence.

    Voltaire has taught me "appreciation is a wonderful thing."

3. Capitalize the first, last and main words of a title.

The main words of a title are the nouns, pronouns, verbs, adjectives, adverbs, and certain conjunctions such as *if, because, as, that, which*.

Rules for capitalizing the small words in the middle of titles vary slightly. A simple rule is not to capitalize prepositions, articles or the conjunctions *and, but, or* and *nor*.

Exception: The first and last words of a title are always capitalized regardless of the type of word.

> Rifles for Watie
>
> The Lion, the Witch and the Wardrobe
>
> The Science of Music

When writing about books, use the same capitalization that is used on the title page of the book, not the cover, because the cover may be written in a style that uses different capitalization than the actual title.

When writing titles for essays, reports or research papers, the following can usually be used as guidelines:

1. Center the title above the text.

2. Leave a blank line between the title and the text.

3. Capitalize the first, last and main words of the title as above.

4. Don't italicize, underline or put your title in quotation marks.

4. Nouns and adjectives that refer to nationalities or ethnic groups, languages, and religions are capitalized.

> Nationalities: French, American, Egyptian, Chinese, Indian
>
> Ethnic groups: Roma, Afrikaners, Cherokee, Arab
>
> Languages: French, Spanish, English, Mandarin, Arabic
>
> Religions: Christianity, Judaism, Islam, Buddhism
>
> Adjectives: French wine, Spanish olive oil, English rose

5. **The usual names for recognized sections of a country are capitalized, even when these include words that wouldn't otherwise be capitalized.**

> Incorrect: He moved from *southern* California to the bay area.
> Correct: He moved from *Southern* California to the Bay Area.
>
> Incorrect: I was born in *west* Texas but grew up in the *midwest*.
> Correct: I was born in *West* Texas but grew up in the *Midwest*.

The names of locations such as streets, highways, cities, parks, buildings, states and countries are also capitalized.

> West Carriage Drive
> Hyde Park
> London, England

Likewise, geographical names such as rivers, mountains, deserts, seas, oceans and islands are capitalized.

> Amazon River
> Rocky Mountains
> Sahara Desert
> Cuba is the largest island in the Caribbean Sea.
> Atlantic Ocean

Direction words, such as *north, south, east, west, northwest, southeast, etc.*, are capitalized when used as a name or part of a name for a location, but not when they indicate a direction.

> He has always lived in the *Northeast*.
>
> Go *northeast* for thirty kilometers until you reach the town of Manchester.

6. **A person's title as well as the names of certain high offices are capitalized.**

> Correct: Reporters go to the White House for press conferences with the *President*.
>
> Correct: *President* Reagan held office for eight years.
>
> Also correct: He interviewed the *president* of the Rotary Club. (The word *president* in this sentence refers to a local club, not a high office.)
>
> Correct: Her grandfather was *Czar* of Russia.
>
> Also correct: The gangster was a known drug *czar*.
>
> Correct: The *Secretary of State* was in an important meeting.
>
> Also correct: The secretary to the company president arranged the meeting.

The words *king, queen, prince* and *princess* are not normally capitalized unless they are part of the title of a specific person, or unless the country is named with the title.

> Correct: She wondered what *Queen* Mary liked to read.
>
> Correct: I would like to introduce the *King* of France.
>
> Also correct: The *queen* was ill that day.

7. **Proper nouns are capitalized; common nouns are not.**

Common nouns are not capitalized, even when they refer to something being written about that seems important.

> Incorrect: Churchill knew the *Country* was in danger of being invaded by Germany.
>
> Correct: Churchill knew the *country* was in danger of being invaded by Germany.
>
> Incorrect: My essay on *Slavery* was very convincing.
>
> Correct: My essay on *slavery* was very convincing.

Incorrect: Many believe that *Capitalism* creates the most prosperous economy.

Correct: Many believe that *capitalism* creates the most prosperous economy.

8. **Days of the week, months, holidays and special events are capitalized. The seasons are not usually capitalized.**

   Correct: Friday   spring
             April   summer
             New Year   fall
             World Cup   winter

9. **Historical periods, events, treaties and documents are capitalized.**

   Correct: Ice Age
             Middle Ages
             Crusades
             Opium Wars
             Magna Carta
             Bill of Rights

10. **In letters and emails, capitalize the first and all other words in a salutation, except small words. Capitalize only the first word in a closing.**

Salutations in personal letters	Salutations in business letters
Dear Annabelle,	Dear Sir:
Dear Sam and Teri,	Dear Madam:
Dear Mr. Jones of Essex County,	Dear Mr. (or Ms.) Romansky:
My Dear Sister,	To Whom It May Concern:

Closings in personal letters

Your friend,

With love,

Till we meet again,

Closings in business letters

Sincerely yours,

Many thanks,

All the best,

Chapter 10
ITALICS AND UNDERLINES

Italics *italics*

1. **Italics are used to indicate the names or titles of books, newspapers, magazines, movies and works of art.**

    Books: *Gone with the Wind*, *The Adventures of Tom Sawyer*

    Newspapers: *The New York Times*, *Dallas Morning News*

    Magazines: *Popular Mechanics*, *Vanity Fair*

    Movies: *Casablanca*, *Singing in the Rain*

    Works of art: The *Mona Lisa*, the *David*

2. **Italics are used to write the names of large vehicles such as ships, trains, aircraft or spacecraft.**

    Ships: The *Titanic* was a British passenger ship that sank on her first voyage.

    Aircraft: *The Spruce Goose* is an enormous airplane built entirely of wood.

    Spacecraft: *Apollo 13* went to the moon and back.

    Trains: We took the *Southwest Chief* from Chicago to Los Angeles.

3. **Italics are used to write words, letters and numbers mentioned as themselves.**

The word *restaurant* is spelled the same in French and English.

The number *seven* is an odd number.

4. **Italics are used to write foreign words in an English sentence.**

She had trained for years to create French *parfums*.

To thank someone in Spanish, say *gracias*.

5. **Italics can be used to emphasize a word or phrase.**

Don't take *that* one.

After tasting some different olive oils, she thought the last one was the best *by far*.

How could you *forget* my birthday?

This use of italics should be done sparingly in formal writing.

Underlines   <u>underline</u>

Underlines serve all the same function as italics. Normally the use of italics is preferred, but in handwriting or word processing where there is no italic font, use underlining instead.

Part 2

GRAMMAR

Chapter 11
A COMMENT ON GRAMMAR

Because grammar can at times be challenging, one might ask: Why do I need to know it?

Grammar is how words are put together to make communication work. You need to know it well enough to understand what you read and to make your writing clear and effective.

Some grammar terms are easy. Some are more challenging. As your reading and writing advance, the need for understanding higher levels of grammar increases.

In Part 2 of this book, there are terms you are probably familiar with, such as noun, pronoun, adverb and preposition. Though common, they are sometimes forgotten. A quick review usually brings the response "Oh, yes, I remember now."

Less common terms that you have probably studied—such as direct object, independent clause and transitive verb—may be more easily forgotten. If you know these terms well, you know grammar better than the average person.

To express more sophisticated ideas, however, you will run into situations where you need to be familiar with higher-level grammar terms; for example, correlative conjunction. Sounds fancy. It's not. It's a conjunction (connecting word, like *and*) made from a pair of words, spaced apart: either-or, neither-nor, both-and. For example, "I will happily eat either Chinese or Mexican for dinner." Tricky-sounding grammar terms are rarely as difficult to understand as they sound.

At the same time, most experienced and successful writers aren't grammar experts. In fact, few could define every term in Part 2 of this book. This might lead you to ask, "Then why are they in a book for high schoolers?"

The answer is simple: Sometimes, you need to know them.

That's why this book is called a handbook. It's designed as a reference you should keep to hand as you work on your writing. There will be times you want to know if a comma is needed, if a word should be capitalized, why a sentence doesn't sound right, or which definition of a word is the one that fits what you are trying to read or write. Getting answers to these questions requires some familiarity with a variety of grammar terms.

When you look up a punctuation point in Part 1, for example, you may need to refer to a grammar term in Part 2 to understand it.

Grammar is useful when you are trying to break down English to understand it better (reading) or to make sure you are understood (writing). There is no other point for grammar. Though some grammar references get quite complex and don't agree with everything in this book, we've done our best to keep the subject simple and useful.

The information presented here is for reference, for your use when needed, not for thorough study and perfect memorization. Use it as a handbook for one purpose only: to get your writing right!

Editors

Chapter 12
ALPHABETICAL REFERENCE OF GRAMMAR TERMS & USAGE

adjective

An adjective is a modifier that describes a noun or a pronoun. It is often next to the word it modifies but not always.

The athletic girl is running in the relay race.
(*Athletic* is an adjective modifying girl.)

Kendall has *many* friends.
(*Many* modifies friends.)

The students are at the *final* ceremony of the year.
(*Final* modifies ceremony.)

adjective incorrectly used as adverb

Use an adverb—not an adjective—to modify a verb.

Incorrect: I want him to go *quick* and see if the mail has come.
Correct: I want him to go *quickly* and see if the mail has come.

Note that in both sentences, *quick* and *quickly* are intended to modify the verb *go*. *Quick* is an adjective, as in "a *quick* action," so it shouldn't be used to modify a verb. Only an adverb can modify a verb, so the adverb *quickly* is correct in this sentence.

> Incorrect: They can't produce food *cheap* enough.
>
> Correct: They can't produce food *cheaply* enough.
>
> Incorrect: The children walked *quiet* to their next class.
>
> Correct: The children walked *quietly* to their next class.

In informal language and casual conversation, the distinction between adjective and adverb is sometimes overlooked. In more formal situations (such as for schoolwork, presentations, or professional speaking or writing), use only adverbs to modify verbs.

> Usage note: *good/well*
>
> *Good* is an adjective and should only be used to modify a noun or pronoun.
>
> *Well* is an adverb that is used to modify a verb. In casual speech good is commonly misused to describe a verb. This is a case of using an adjective incorrectly as an adverb and is not accepted in professional speech or writing.
>
> Informal: I am doing *good*.
>
> Formal: I am doing *well*.
>
> Informal: "How ya doin'?"
>
> "Good, thanks!"
>
> Formal: "How are you doing?"
>
> "Well, thanks!"

adjective phrase

See "phrase" on page 98.

adverb

An adverb is a modifier that describes or limits a verb or another modifier (adjective or adverb).

Adverbs that modify a verb:

We rowed the boat *quickly*.
(*Quickly* modifies the verb *rowed*.)

Jason *often* forgets his homework.
(*Often* modifies *forgets*.)

The ship to Shanghai sailed *away*.
(*Away* modifies *sailed*.)

That dog should *not* leave the yard.
(The adverb *not* means "to no extent, in no way." *Not* modifies the verbs *should leave*.)

Adverbs that modify an adjective:

The house was *completely* dirty.
(*Completely* is an adverb that modifies the adjective *dirty*.)

There are *too* many people in the elevator.
(The adjective *many* modifies *people*. *Too* modifies *many*.)

Jenny and Paul are *frequently* late.
(*Frequently* is an adverb that modifies *late*.)

Adverbs that modify another adverb:

Race car drivers go *very* fast.
(*Fast* is an adverb that modifies the verb *go*. *Very* is an adverb that modifies the adverb *fast*.)

We hear bad news *much too* often.
(*Often* is an adverb that modifies the verb *hear*. *Too* is an adverb that modifies the adverb *often*. *Much* is an adverb that modifies the adverb *too*. It isn't just *too* often, but *much* too often.)

The photographer took six photos *really quickly* and left.
(*Quickly* is an adverb that modifies the verb *took*. *Really* is an adverb that modifies the adverb *quickly* but is only used in informal speech.)

adverb clause

See "clause" on page 69.

adverb phrase

See "phrase" on page 98.

antecedent

An antecedent is the word a pronoun is taking the place of. It usually comes before the pronoun. (From Latin *ante,* "before" + *cedere,* "to go.")

Example:

          antecedent   pronoun
When my *girlfriend* arrived, *she* was ready to study.

Make pronouns agree with their antecedents.

Incorrect: When my friends arrived, *she* was ready to study.

Correct: When my friends arrived, *they* were ready to study.

Refer clearly to antecedents.

Incorrect (unclear): The daughter of Ms. Smythe, who went to Boston College, drank green tea.
(Who went to Boston College? The daughter or Ms. Smythe?)

Correct (clear): Ms. Smythe's daughter, who went to Boston College, drank green tea.

Incorrect (unclear): The Student Council proposal for the dress code, debated for weeks, is well written.
(Was the proposal or the dress code debated for weeks?)

Correct (clear): After weeks of debate concerning the dress code, the Student Council submitted a well-written proposal revising it.

appositive

An appositive is a word or group of words acting as a noun to explain, rename or identify a previously stated noun or pronoun.

Please keep an eye on my favorite dog, *Sierra*.
(*Sierra* is the appositive. It renames the previous noun, dog.)

Annie will help you load the car, *the Mercedes parked in front*.
(*The Mercedes parked in front* is the appositive. It is a phrase that identifies the *car*.)

Rebecca gave the book to Jerry, *the one who should have gotten it before*.
(*The one who should have gotten it before* is the appositive. It is a group of words that explains who *Jerry* is.)

article

The three words *a, an* and *the* are called articles. An article is a type of adjective.

1. *A* and *an* both mean "one thing without saying which particular thing." *A* is used before words starting with a consonant sound. *An* is used before words starting with a vowel sound. (See "article usage" on page 64, for more on this.)

   I bought *a* book.

   (It means you bought just one book but not saying which particular book.)

   Andy chose *an* apple for dessert.

2. *The* means one or more specified things.

> *The* bicycles need to be fixed.
> (*The* shows that particular bicycles are being talked about.)

> George Washington fought in *the* American Revolution.

> They bought *the* best trees at *the* garden center.

article usage

Use *an* instead of *a* before a vowel sound, including the vowel sound that begins with a silent *h*.

> **Incorrect:** Aubrey caught *a* ant in the garden.
>
> **Correct:** Aubrey caught *an* ant in the garden.
>
> **Incorrect:** Diogenes couldn't find *a* honest man.
>
> **Correct:** Diogenes couldn't find *an* honest man.

Some words begin with vowels that have a consonant sound. In this case, use *a* not *an*.

> **Incorrect:** I want to know how much *an* euro is worth.
> (This is incorrect because euro begins with a y consonant sound.)
>
> **Correct:** I want to know how much *a* euro is worth.

When *the* is written before a noun with a vowel sound, it is spelled the same.

C

case

Case refers to the job or function a noun or pronoun has in a sentence:

> subject (nominative case)
> > The *dog* licked my face. (subject)
>
> object (objective case)
> > He petted the *dog*. (direct object)
> > He sat by the *dog*. (object of a preposition)
> > I gave my *dog* a bone. (indirect object)
>
> possession (possessive case)
> > That is my *dog's* bone.

cases of pronouns

Unlike nouns, most pronouns change form depending on whether they are acting as the subject, acting as an object, or showing possession.

When a pronoun functions as a subject, it is in the nominative case.

> *We* like apples.

(*We* is the subject. *We* is in the nominative case.)

When a pronoun acts as an object, whether it's a direct object, indirect object or the object of a preposition, it is in the objective case.

> The burglar attacked *us*.

(*Us* is a direct object. *Us* is in the objective case.)

When a pronoun shows possession, it is in the possessive case.

That boat is *ours*.

(*Ours* shows possession. *Ours* is in the possessive case.)

The cases of pronouns are shown here:

nominative case	objective case	possessive case
I	*me*	*mine*
you	*you*	*yours*
he	*him*	*his*
she	*her*	*hers*
it	*it*	*its*
we	*us*	*ours*
they	*them*	*theirs*
who	*whom*	*whose*

1. Nominative case pronouns

    Incorrect: Sophia and *me* are going to the library now.
    Correct: Sophia and *I* are going to the library now.

    (You would not say, "*Me* is going to the library now." You would say, "I am going to the library now.")

    Incorrect: *Them* are playing a tough match today.
    Correct: *They* are playing a tough match today.

    Incorrect: *Whom* wants chocolate?
    Correct: *Who* wants chocolate?

2. Objective case pronouns

    direct object

    Incorrect: You kissed *she* right on the lips!
    Correct: You kissed *her* right on the lips!

indirect object

Incorrect: My father gave my brother and *I* flying lessons.
Correct: My father gave my brother and *me* flying lessons.

(You would not say, "My father gave I flying lessons." You would say, "My father gave me flying lessons.")

object of a preposition

Incorrect: He wanted to talk to Joe and *I*.
Correct: He wanted to talk to Joe and *me*.

(You would not say, "He wanted to talk to I." You would say, "He wanted to talk to me.")

3. Possessive case pronouns

That computer is *mine*. Which one is *yours*?

Hers is the one with the pink stickers on it.

cases of nouns

Nouns don't change in the nominative case and objective case.

The *burglar* attacked us.	(nominative)
We attacked the *burglar*.	(objective)
The *dog* chased the cat.	(nominative)
The *cat* chased the dog.	(objective)

Nouns do change in the possessive case, usually by adding 's.

Bryce's goal
the *lion's* roar
a *day's* work

When a singular noun ends in *s* or *z*, you still add *'s*.

> the dress's colors
>
> the gas's price

You will occasionally find the *s* omitted when it is a name ending in an *s* or *z* sound, though both are accepted.

> Thomas's class   or   Thomas' class
>
> Roz's house   or   Roz' house

For ancient and biblical names of more than one syllable ending in *s*, the *s* is usually omitted.

> Jesus' disciples
>
> Socrates' writing
>
> Zeus's thunderbolt   (one syllable)

To form the possessive for a plural noun that doesn't end in s, add an apostrophe and an *s*.

> the children's hour
>
> the oxen's feed
>
> the geese's nests

To form the possessive for a plural noun ending in *s*, simply add an apostrophe at the end.

> the employees' parking lot

A period of time or amount of money can be thought of as having something. These possessives are formed the same way, with an apostrophe and *s*.

> a moment's consideration
>
> a week's vacation
>
> twelve cents' worth of paper
>
> a dollar's worth of gas

clause

A clause is a group of words that has a subject and its verb. It is often part of a larger sentence. There are two basic clauses, independent and dependent.

independent clause

An independent clause expresses a complete thought. It can be part of a larger sentence, or it can stand alone as a simple sentence.

                      subject   verb
The volleyball team played its first game in the new gymnasium.

subject verb
Tomas plays basketball.

                          subject   verb
Despite losing, the team had played their best game.

dependent clause

A dependent clause has a subject and its verb but does not express a complete thought and cannot stand alone. It depends on an independent clause to complete its meaning.

Because it started raining,

(This dependent clause doesn't make sense by itself. Join it with an independent clause and it makes sense.)

Because it started raining, the baseball team couldn't finish its game.

      subject verb   subject verb
If the rain stops, we can go to the beach.
      dependent clause   independent clause

subject verb   subject verb
We visited our friends when we were in Paris.
  independent clause   dependent clause

subject verb   subject verb
Joseph is a student who is always on time.
  independent clause   dependent clause

A dependent clause acts as an adjective, adverb or noun.

1. adjective clause

    An adjective clause is a dependent clause that modifies a noun or pronoun. It usually starts with *that, which, who, whom* or *whose*.

    I have a sister *who is younger than me.*
    (adjective clause modifies *sister*)

    The woman, *whom you met earlier,* is Headmistress of this school.
    (adjective clause modifies *woman*)

    I spilled something on the jacket *that I wore to the movies.*
    (adjective clause modifies *jacket*)

2. adverb clause

    An adverb clause is a dependent clause that modifies a verb. It usually starts with a subordinating conjunction, examples of which are shown here:

    | *after* | *although* | *as* |
    | *as if* | *as though* | *as long as* |
    | *because* | *before* | *if* |
    | *in order that* | *since* | *so that* |
    | *than* | *though* | *unless* |
    | *until* | *when* | *whenever* |
    | *where* | *wherever* | *while* |

    Because it started raining, the baseball team couldn't finish their game.
    (adverb clause modifies the verb phrase *couldn't finish*)

    We studied *until we completed all the research we needed.*
    (adverb clause modifies the verb *studied*)

    The deer wandered *when food became more difficult to find.*
    (adverb clause modifies the verb *wandered*)

3. noun clause

A noun clause is a dependent clause that serves the role of a noun in a sentence. It can be a subject, direct object, indirect object, object of a preposition or noun restatement.

What the newspaper reported was inaccurate.
(subject)

The fashion designer knows *why her new fashions are so popular.*
(direct object)

The driver gave *whoever needed one* a ride to the tournament.
(indirect object)

Gardeners notice the plants all *around them.*
(object of a preposition)

Roberto, *who is student council president,* made the proposal to the Headmaster.
(noun restatement)

The runner's greatest dream was *that he would one day win Olympic gold.*
(noun restatement)

clause, restrictive and nonrestrictive

1. A restrictive clause is a dependent clause that gives specific data about the person or thing being written about in a sentence. It provides essential information that distinguishes that person or thing from any other. For this reason, it can also be called an essential clause.

   The French city *that I enjoy the most* is Paris.

   The dog *that I chose* was the friendliest one in the litter.

   When I was learning to sail, I used the only sailboat *that was available.*

   Here is the box *that has all our family photographs.*

2. A nonrestrictive clause, on the other hand, is a dependent clause that isn't essential to the meaning of the sentence. It simply adds some data. Thus, it is often called a nonessential clause.

Generally, nonrestrictive clauses are set off with commas, which shows that the clause provides nonessential information.

The largest city in Scotland, *which I have visited twice*, is Glasgow.

The smartest breed of dog is the Border Collie, *which is usually black and white in color.*

I learned ocean sailing in a small, wooden sailboat, *which was one of many built in Rhode Island.*

In 1985, *when all the photographs in this box were taken,* my father used a film camera.

Restrictive clauses, however, are not set off with commas. The added information is essential, and the sentence wouldn't make full sense without it.

The largest city in Scotland *that I've visited* is Glasgow.

The smartest dog the trainer had ever worked with was the Border Collie *that the Yoshida family brought to her.*

I learned ocean sailing in a small, wooden sailboat *that my uncle gave me.*

All the photographs *that you will find in this box* were taken by my father with his film camera.

colloquial language

This is language used mainly in conversation or informal writing, such as a personal email or letter. Colloquial language should be avoided in formal writing or speaking.

Examples of colloquial language:

fun as an adjective

That was a *fun* trip.

alright to mean all right

Alright, I'll be there.

kid to mean a child or any young person

There were kids everywhere.

When in doubt if a word is colloquial or not, check a dictionary. If a word or usage is labeled "colloquial," "informal," "slang" (very informal) or "vulgar" (rude, offensive or indecent), it should be avoided in academic or professional writing.

complete subject

See "subject" on page 114.

compound modifier

Two or more modifiers that act together to modify a noun as if they were a single adjective. (See Part 1, chapter 8, for guidelines on when to use a hyphen with a compound modifier.)

The bird soared through the *cloud-dotted* sky.

The *heavily used* copy machine had to be replaced.

compound sentence

A sentence with two or more independent clauses joined by a coordinating conjunction.

He's a good tennis player, and he rides a horse well.

She doesn't like to bake desserts, but she loves to cook dinners.

compound subject

See "subject" on page 114.

conjunction

A word used to join words or groups of words.

Examples:

brush *and* paint
(*and* joins two words)

across the field *but* not the river
(*but* joins two phrases)

She thought she might travel the world, *or* she would start college next year.
(*or* joins two clauses)

There are three types of conjunctions:

1. A conjunction that joins similar words or groups of words is a coordinating conjunction.

   I sent her flowers *and* candy.
   (The word *and* connects two nouns.)

   Anna was quiet *yet* wiser than most girls her age.
   (The word *yet* joins two modifiers.)

   Bobby went home *but* Anya stayed at the party.
   (The word *but* joins two similar statements.)

   And, but and *or* are the most common coordinating conjunctions. The full list of this type is here: *for, and, nor, but, or, yet* and *so*. A trick for remembering all the coordinating conjunctions is the word FANBOYS, which is made using the first letter of each.

2. A conjunction that is a pair of words to join equal elements of a sentence is a correlative conjunction. These conjunctions are *either...or, neither...nor, both...and,* and *not only...but also.*

   She is planning to go to Indonesia to teach *either* English *or* French.

   Professional musicians need *not only* hours of practice *but also* many skills with their instruments.

Neither the juniors *nor* the seniors could solve the Headmaster's riddle.

3. A conjunction that is a word or words used to introduce an adverb clause is a subordinating conjunction.

    After Marcella finished her homework, she wrote a song for her best friend.
    (*After* is the conjunction that introduces the adverb clause *After Marcella finished her homework*. It is an adverb clause because it tells when she wrote a song.)

    Because Ray was running a marathon the next day, he went to sleep early.
    (*Because* is the conjunction that introduces the adverb clause *Because Ray was running a marathon the next day*. It is an adverb clause because it tells why he went to sleep early.)

    Since she wanted that job, Misty studied and prepared for the job interview.
    (*Since* is the conjunction that introduces the adverb clause *Since she wanted that job*. It is an adverb clause because it tells why Misty studied and prepared for the job interview.)

    Here are the words most commonly used as this type of conjunction:

    | *after* | *although* | *as* |
    | *as if* | *as though* | *as long as* |
    | *because* | *before* | *if* |
    | *in order that* | *since* | *so that* |
    | *than* | *though* | *unless* |
    | *until* | *when* | *whenever* |
    | *where* | *wherever* | *while* |

coordinating conjunction

See "conjunction" on page 74.

contraction

A contraction is a word formed by omitting letters from a word or group of words and substituting an apostrophe for what is omitted.

    can't   (cannot)

    what's   (what is)

    flyin'   (flying—informal)

    e'er   (ever—poetic)

On occasion, a contraction is formed by changing some letters, for example:

    won't   (will not)

Though contractions are avoided in very formal writing, such as legal documents, most common contractions are acceptable in formal writing if not overused. Some teachers and professors frown on their use, however—particularly, in research papers.

correlative conjunction

See "conjunction" on page 74.

dependent clause

See "clause" on page 69.

direct object

A noun or pronoun that tells the goal or result of the verb in a sentence. A direct object tells exactly what the action of the verb is directed to, performed on, or resulted in. A sentence can have more than one direct object, or it can have none.

> Ira sent a *letter*.
>
> The chemistry experiment proved the *presence* of an acid.
>
> Shaun hit the *target* in the center.
>
> She uses her *computer* and *scanner* every day.
>
> The drama club performed a short *play* every other Friday.

When a sentence has a being verb, there is no action taking place so there is no direct object.

> She is the president of the chess club.
> (*President* is not a direct object. It is a noun restatement, a word that says what she is, not what she does or acts upon.)
>
> He became a doctor after years of training.
> (*Doctor* is not a direct object. It is a noun restatement that says what he became, not what he did or acted upon.)

e

essential clause

See "clause, restrictive and nonrestrictive" on page 71.

f

future perfect tense

See "perfect tenses" on page 93.

g

gerund

A grammar term less often used, it simply refers to a verb form ending in *–ing* that acts as a noun.

> Examples:
>
> *Swimming is good exercise.*
> (*Swimming* is a gerund. It acts as a noun, the subject of the sentence.)
>
> *Celia loves reading.*
> (*Reading* is a gerund. It acts as a noun, the direct object of the verb *loves*.)

Riding a horse in Olympic competition takes years of *training*.
(Both *Riding* and *training* are gerunds. The first acts as a noun, the subject of the sentence. The second acts as a noun, the object of the preposition *of*.)

helping verb

A verb that helps the main verb in a verb phrase. (Also called an auxiliary verb.)

Joelle *is driving* to town.
(*Is* helps the main verb *driving* in the verb phrase *is driving*.)

I *am hoping* we *can go* tomorrow.
(*Am* helps the main verb *hoping*. *Can* helps *go*.)

The goats crossed the river and *are* now *climbing* the mountain.
(*Are* helps *climbing* in the verb phrase *are climbing*.)

Is she *trying* to make you angry?
(*Is* helps *trying* in the verb phrase *is trying*.)

Frederic *might forget* your name—he usually *does*.
(*Might* helps *forget*. *Does* helps *forget* also, even though the word *forget* is not used the second time because the reader knows "he usually *does forget*" is meant.)

Do you *think* we *will be studying* tonight?
(*Do* helps *think*. *Will* and *be* both help *studying*.)

I

imperative mood

See "mood (or mode) of verbs" on page 83.

independent clause

See "clause" on page 69.

indicative mood

See "mood (or mode) of verbs" on page 83.

indirect object

A direct object is the noun or pronoun that tells the goal or result of the verb in a sentence. The indirect object tells who or what the action of the verb is being done to or done for. It answers the question—*Who* or *what* is the action done to or done for?

A sentence can only have an indirect object when there is also a direct object. The indirect object always precedes the direct object.

                              indirect obj   direct obj
My grandmother gave   *me*   some cookies.

                              indirect obj   direct obj
Rohan and Samar taught *themselves* arithmetic when they were young.

                       indirect obj   direct obj
The sailor gave his *boat* a new   coat of paint.

infinitive

The basic form of a verb. Like "infinite," *infinitive* means "without limit" because the infinitive expresses a verb's action or state of being, without limiting it to a tense or person.

The infinitive form of the verb can be written with or without a *to* in front; for example, the infinitive of *work* can be written *to work* or just *work*.

When the word *to* is used with the infinitive, it has no meaning; it simply shows that the verb is in the infinitive form.

The infinitive form of a verb is sometimes called the root or base form.

to be, be

to have, have

to play, play

to sing, sing

interjection

An interjection is a word that expresses strong or sudden emotion. An exclamation mark is often used with an interjection.

Hurray! Our team won.

Ouch! You stepped on my foot.

Really! That's very good news.

Help! I've twisted my ankle.

intransitive verb

See "verb, transitive and intransitive" on page 121.

J

jobs that nouns and pronouns do

See "nouns and pronouns, jobs in a sentence" on page 89.

M

modifier

A modifier is a word or group of words in a sentence that describes or limits the meaning of something else in a sentence. Adjectives and adverbs are both modifiers.

> The *old, red* barn was falling *down*.

---

modifier placement

To make your meaning clear, place a modifier next to whatever it modifies.

> **Different meaning due to placement of the modifier *only*:**
>
> *Only* he will eat vegetables.
> (He is the only person who will eat vegetables.)
>
> He will eat *only* vegetables.
> (He won't eat other things, only vegetables.)
>
> Unclear: *After shuffling along exhaustedly,* I saw the old man slump to his knees.
> (Was I shuffling along exhaustedly or was the old man?)

Clear: *After shuffling along exhaustedly,* the old man slumped to his knees.
(The modifying phrase now clearly modifies *old man.*)

Unclear: *To type without strain,* your keyboard must be positioned correctly.
(Are we trying to get the keyboard free of strain?)

Clear: *To type without strain,* you must position your keyboard correctly.
(With the modifier placed next to *you*, it is now clear.)

---

mood (or mode) of verbs

A verb shows something called *mood*. This definition does not refer to how a person feels but whether the verb's action or state of being is given as a fact, a command, or a wish or possibility.

There are three moods used in English:

1. Indicative mood

This mood is used for factual, ordinary statements or questions. Most verbs are used in this mood.

> He *plays* on the soccer team.
>
> Which team do you *play* next week?

2. Imperative mood

Used to show a command or request.

> *Play* harder today!
>
> Joseph, please *stop* bothering your sister.

3. Subjunctive mood

The subjunctive mood is used to express a wish, a possibility or a condition (such as something imagined or something that depends on something else).

The most common verbs in subjunctive mood are those that express a possibility, such as these: *could, may, might, should, ought to.*[2]

Possibility (subjunctive): I *could walk* ten miles tomorrow.

Fact (indicative): I *will walk* ten miles tomorrow.

Possibility: We *may take* a trip this summer.

Fact: We *will take* a trip this summer.

Possibility: Frieda *might win* the contest this year.

Fact: Frieda *will win* the contest this year.

Possibility: I think *we should* leave soon.

Fact: I think we *will leave* soon.

Possibility: The team *ought to arrive* any minute.

Fact: The team *will arrive* any minute.

It is also common for the subjunctive to express a condition, using *would* or *should*.

Condition (subjunctive): I *would go* if I had the money.

Fact (indicative): I *will go* now that I have the money.

Condition: *Should* you *be* willing to join me, I *would* really *like* to go.

Fact: Since you *are* willing to join me, I really *want* to go.

Along with expressing wish, the subjunctive mood can be used to show that something is an expectation or the proper thing to do.

Wish (subjunctive): I suggest she *do* the cooking tonight.

Fact (indicative): She *does* the cooking tonight.

---

2 Many grammar references call these verbs (*could, may, might, should, ought to* and *would*) "modal verbs." What's important and agreed upon is that they are helping verbs expressing possibility or condition.

Proper (subjunctive): It is important that he *study* hard to pass.

Fact (indicative): It is important that he *studies hard. That's why he's passing.*

Notice in the last examples, when used alone without a helping verb (such as *could* or *may*), verbs in the subjunctive mood are usually in the third person, singular form without the *–s* or *-es*. See "person (first, second, third)" on page 96. Here are more examples:

Proper (subjunctive): It is only right that he *go* with us.

Fact (indicative): He *goes* with us.

Wish (subjunctive): I *would hope* that he *ask* his father first.

Fact (indicative): He *will ask* his father first.

The verb *be* changes to a different form in the subjunctive mood—*is* and *was* become *be* and *were*.

Expectation (subjunctive): It is important that everyone *be* on time.

Fact (indicative): Everyone *is* on time.

Wish (subjunctive): I *would prefer* that he *be* the leader of this project.

Fact (indicative): He *is* the leader of this project.

Condition (subjunctive): If I *were* an artist, I *would paint* what I wished.

Fact (indicative): When I *was* an artist, I *painted* what I wished.

Wish (subjunctive): I wish I *were* going to the movies instead of studying.

Fact (indicative): I *was going* to the movies instead of studying.

nominative case

See "case" on page 65.

nonessential clause

See "clause, restrictive and nonrestrictive" on page 71.

nonrestrictive clause

See "clause, restrictive and nonrestrictive" on page 71.

noun

A noun is a word that names a person, place, thing or idea.

> The *girls* from *Greece* warmed themselves by the *fire*.
>
> This gave them some *comfort*.
>
> *Women* around the *world* celebrated a *day* devoted to their *empowerment*.

noun clause

See "clause" on page 69.

noun, collective

A collective noun names a group of people, places, things or ideas. *Family, choir, audience* and *team* are collective nouns that each name a group of people. *Library, swarm, flock* and *galaxy* are collective nouns that name groups of things.

Collective nouns have both singular and plural forms:

>one family, two families

>one choir, two choirs

>one audience, two audiences

A singular collective noun, such as *mob, army, team, group, crowd* is treated as a singular subject so it takes a singular verb. The same applies to numerical words or phrases, for example, *number, majority, five dollars, twelve days*.

>**Incorrect:** My team *are* a great bunch of guys.
>
>**Correct:** My team *is* a great bunch of guys.
>
>**Incorrect:** Five dollars *are* too much for that pen.
>
>**Correct:** Five dollars *is* too much for that pen.

A plural collective noun takes a plural verb.

>**Incorrect:** The two teams *is* playing again in the championship game.
>
>**Correct:** The two teams *are* playing again in the championship game.

---

noun phrase

See "phrase" on page 98.

noun, proper

A proper noun is the actual name of a person, place or thing. Proper nouns always begin with a capital letter.

> Minji Kim
> Richard Bailey
> Rex
> United States
> France
> Southwest Airlines
> Kleenex

---

noun restatement

Restate means to state again in a different way. A noun restatement is a second noun or pronoun that restates, renames or identifies a previously stated noun or pronoun in a sentence. (These are also called appositives.)

Many noun restatements immediately follow the noun or pronoun they restate.

> Please keep an eye on my dog, *Frankie*.
> After lunch, we will meet my brother, *Bob*.
> Rebecca gave the book to Jerry, her next-door *neighbor*.
> "Hi, it's me—your favorite *cousin*!"

A noun restatement that renames the subject of a sentence is a subject restatement. (These are sometimes called predicate nominatives.) In this case, it always follows a being verb or verb phrase such as: *is, am, was, were, will be, becomes, became, is being, is becoming.*

> After all, Jemma is the smartest *dog* in town.
> Our best players are *Hailey* and *Jia*.
> Her sister is a famous *ballerina*.
> She became *President* of the United States of America.

nouns and pronouns, jobs in a sentence

There are five jobs that nouns and pronouns can do in a sentence, listed below. Each is covered under its own entry in this book.

1. subject
2. direct object
3. indirect object
4. object of a preposition
5. noun restatement

objective case

See "case" on page 65.

---

object of a preposition

The object of a preposition is the noun or pronoun that is affected by the preposition it follows. The group of words starting with the preposition and ending with the object is called a prepositional phrase.

She typed *on her computer.*
(*On* is the preposition. *On her computer* is the prepositional phrase and *computer* is the object of the preposition.)

They were studying *in the library.*
(*In* is the preposition. *In the library* is the prepositional phrase and *library* is the object of the preposition.)

The book is *under the chair.*
(*Under* is the preposition. *Under the chair* is the prepositional phrase and *chair* is the object of the preposition.)

The preposition is what shows the relationship between its object and whatever the prepositional phrase is modifying.

She typed *on her computer.*
(*On her computer* modifies *typed*, telling where it occurred.)

They were studying *in the library.*
(*In the library* modifies *studying*, telling where.)

The book is *under the chair.*
(*Under the chair* modifies *is*, telling where.)

The event starts *at ten-thirty.*
(*At ten-thirty* modifies *starts*, telling when.)

parallel structure

Also called parallelism, parallel structure means writing coordinated ideas (ideas of equal importance) in the same form. Writing is easier to read and understand when the coordinated ideas in a sentence are written in the same form.

Here are examples of times parallel structure comes into play:

1. It is used when writing a series of words or phrases.

    Incorrect: On our trip we *hiked, did some swimming, and water skiing.*

    Correct: On our trip we went *hiking, swimming and water skiing.*

    Incorrect: We will fight them *on the land, seas* and *in the air.*

    Correct: We will fight them *on the land, on the seas* and *in the air.*

2. Parallel structure is also used when writing with pairs of conjunctions. The conjunctions are placed right before the parallel items.

   Incorrect: To lift the heavy box, they tried *both* leverage *and* to force it up.

   Correct: To lift the heavy box, they tried *both* leverage *and* force.

   (*Leverage* is a noun, so *force* is also a noun.)

   Incorrect: I will *either* teach the class myself *or* someone else I arrange will.

   Correct: I will *either* teach that class *or* arrange for someone else to teach it.

   (*Either* is followed by a verb, so *or* is also followed by a verb.)

3. Parallel structure is used when comparing or contrasting ideas.

   Incorrect: His photography was praised more for *how well he showed its subjects* than *its quality*.

   Correct: His photography was praised more for *its subjects* than *its quality*.

   Incorrect: I am more interested in *cars* than *riding motorcycles*.

   Correct: I am more interested in *cars* than *motorcycles*.

   Correct: I am more interested *in driving cars* than *in riding motorcycles*.

---

participle

A participle is a verb form. It is usually formed by adding *–ing* (*present participle*) or *–ed* (*past participle*) to the basic verb.

basic verb	present participle	past participle
talk	talking	talked
hike	hiking	hiked

A participle is used two ways:

1. As an adjective, usually before the noun it modifies.

    The *swimming* dolphins played at the side of our boat.

    She only eats *cooked* seafood.

    The pirates found *buried* treasure on the *deserted* island.

    When a participle comes after the noun it modifies, it is harder to recognize it as a modifier and easier to mistake it for a verb.

    The diners could hear plates *breaking* as someone fell in the kitchen.
    (*Breaking* modifies the noun *plates*.)

    There were many more letters *sent* yesterday.
    (*Sent* modifies the noun *letters*.)

    Who are the people *going* first?
    (*Going* modifies the noun *people*.)

2. With a form of *be* or *have* to form certain verb tenses.

    The girls *have been swimming* all afternoon.

    They *had cooked* a lovely meal for their guests.

    The pirates *were burying* their treasure so no one else could find it.

Some verbs have different forms for the past participle. These are called *irregular* verbs. Here are some examples:

basic verb	present participle	past participle
eat	eating	eaten
bring	bringing	brought
swim	swimming	swum

For more examples, see "Irregular Verbs" on page 135.

participle phrase

See "phrase" on page 98.

past participle

See "participle" on page 91.

past perfect tense

See "perfect tenses" on page 93.

perfect tenses

Perfect tenses are used to talk or write about an action or state of being that has been completed. There are perfect tenses for the past, present and future, as shown below.

1. Present perfect

Shows an action or state of being that happened in the past but has been completed by the present. It is formed with *has* or *have* plus the past participle.

> I *have read* that book.
>
> We *have succeeded* in winning all our games.
>
> The tiger *has eaten* its prey.
>
> John enjoys writing; in fact, he *has written* three books in the last two years.
>
> Mr. O'Connor is a close friend and *has been* for several years now.

2. Past perfect

Shows an action or state of being that happened and was completed before a particular point in the past. It is formed with *had* plus the past participle.

Our teacher *had called* your name by the time you arrived.

When you saw me, I *had* just *arrived* back from Africa.

Before he made the basket, the buzzer *had sounded,* ending the game.

I *had eaten* before the party, so I left my piece of cake untouched.

When I arrived home, my mother said I looked like I *had played* soccer all day.

3. Future perfect

Shows an action or state of being that will be completed at some future time. It is formed with *will have* or *shall have* plus the past participle.

By tomorrow, I *will have finished* my painting.

I'd love to join you Saturday for dinner, but I *will have left* for Ireland by then.

Mrs. Sweet w*ill have finished* the project before summer comes around.

Our group *will have performed* before Silvia has recovered from her broken leg.

The pilot *will have passed* his test before taking passengers on his plane.

perfect progressive tenses

The perfect progressive tenses are used to talk about an action or state of being that continued for a period of time and then completed.

There are three perfect progressive tenses: present perfect progressive, past perfect progressive and future perfect progressive.

1. Present perfect progressive

Shows an action or state of being continuing up to the present. It is formed with a verb phrase using *has been* or *have been* + the present participle.

Use the present progressive tense to talk about an activity that has just stopped or about actions that are repeated over a period of time up to now.

> I *have been studying* all day.
>
> You're out of breath. *Have* you *been exercising*?
>
> We *have been traveling* for the past two days.
>
> It *has been raining* all day, so the ground is muddy.
>
> John *has been competing* in tennis tournaments since he was ten years old.

2. Past perfect progressive

Shows an action or state of being that was continued for some period of time in the past and then it was completed. It is formed with a verb phrase using *had been* + the present participle.

Use the past perfect progressive tense to talk about something that *had been happening* for some period before something else happened.

> I *had been studying* until midnight for a month, but that ended when I stopped last week.
>
> We *had been skiing* in the sun all morning, but that ended when it started to snow after lunch.
>
> Sylvie was resting because she *had been working* hard in the garden.

3. Future perfect progressive

Shows an action or state of being that is continuing until sometime in the future, then it will be complete. It uses *will* + *have been* + the present participle.

> By 5 p.m., the girls *will have been jumping* rope all afternoon.

> Next month, I *will have been riding* horses for twenty years.

> By tomorrow, it *will have been snowing* steadily for three days.

For more examples, see "Verb Tenses" on page 137.

---

person (first, second, third)

There are different pronouns used depending on the person or persons being talked about. There are singular and plural forms of each.

1. First person

When talking about yourself, you use the following pronouns:

singular	plural
I	we
me	us
myself	ourselves
mine	ours

> *I* am often forgetful.

> *We* are leaving tomorrow.

> She gave the car to *me*.

> This book is *ours*.

2. Second person

When talking to someone, you use the following pronouns:

singular	plural
you	*you*
yourself	*yourselves*
yours	*yours*

You are often forgetful.

Are all of *you* leaving tomorrow?

Speak for *yourself*.

This book is *yours*.

3. Third person

When talking about another person or other people, you use the following pronouns:

singular	plural
he	*they*
she	*they*
it	*they*
him	*them*
her	*them*
his	*theirs*
hers	*theirs*
its	*theirs*
himself	*themselves*
herself	*themselves*
itself	*themselves*

He is often forgetful.

Is *she* leaving tomorrow?

They are speaking for *themselves*.

I haven't seen *it*.

Note that the plural versions of third person pronouns are increasingly used as singular when the gender is unknown or unimportant.

> If a teacher is tough, do *they* give students more homework?

As of this book's publication, most writers and editors suggest rewriting sentences to avoid using *they, them*, etc., as singular pronouns, if possible.

> If teachers are tough, do *they* give students more homework?
>
> Does giving students more homework mean a teacher is tough? (no pronoun)

In the past, when the gender was unknown or unimportant, using the masculine form was the standard.

> If a teacher is tough, does *he* give students more homework?

phrase

A group of two or more words that act like a single part of speech in a sentence. It can contain a subject or a verb but not both. The common types of phrases are explained below.

1. Adjective phrase

An adjective phrase is a prepositional phrase that serves to modify a noun or pronoun in a sentence.

> The books *in the classroom* are new.
>
> Many *of the students* are studying history this month.
>
> Those *on the soccer team* will play their next game tomorrow.

2. Adverb phrase

An adverb phrase is a phrase that serves to modify a verb or another modifier in a sentence.

> Susan hit the softball *over all the outfielders.*
>
> She performs every concert *with all her heart and soul.*
>
> Jon left the dentist *very quickly.*

3. Noun phrase

A noun phrase acts as a noun in a sentence and contains a verb form ending in *–ing*.

Telling my parents was the honest thing to do.

My favorite sport in the summer is *swimming in races.*

Finding the ideal career is the goal of many college students today.

4. Participle phrase

This is a phrase that starts with a participle. It acts as an adjective to modify a noun or pronoun in a sentence.

Removing his shoes, Clive dove into the lake to help the children swim.

Buried for four hundred years, the statue was damaged but intact.

In New Orleans, an entire neighborhood *destroyed by flooding* had to be rebuilt.

5. Prepositional phrase

A prepositional phrase is a group of words that begins with a preposition and ends with one or more nouns or pronouns. It acts as either an adjective or adverb in a sentence.

The yearbook *of her high school years* showed all her favorite activities.
(acts as adjective modifying *yearbook*)

The train went *through the beautiful French countryside.*
(acts as adverb modifying *went* by saying where)

After the movie, they rushed to eat dinner.
(acts as adverb modifying *rushed* by saying when)

She was intelligent *to the highest degree.*
(acts as adverb modifying the adjective *intelligent*)

He threw the ball close *to the referee.*
(acts as adverb modifying the adverb *close*)

phrase, restrictive and nonrestrictive

A restrictive phrase gives specific data about the person or thing being written about in a sentence. It provides essential information that distinguishes that person or thing from any other. (For this reason, it is also called an essential phrase.)

Restrictive phrases are not set off with commas. The added information is essential to the basic meaning of the sentence.

> The French city *of my choice* is Rouen.
>
> The duck *swimming in the pond* belongs to Paco.
>
> When I was learning to sail, I took lessons *from Captain Ian.*
>
> Here is the box *containing all our family photographs.*

A nonrestrictive phrase isn't essential to the meaning of the sentence. It simply adds some data. (Also called a nonessential phrase.)

Nonrestrictive phrases are set off by commas.

> The busiest city in Scotland, *not including Glasgow,* is Edinburgh.
>
> The smartest breed of dog is the Border Collie, *often black and white in color.*
>
> I learned ocean sailing in a small sailboat, *built in Rhode Island.*
>
> In the 80s and 90s, *before digital cameras,* my father used a film camera to take all our family photographs.

possessive case

See "case" on page 65.

predicate nominative

See "noun restatement" on page 88.

preposition

A preposition is a word used to show the relationship (often in physical direction or time) between a noun or pronoun following it and another word in the sentence.

The group of words formed is called a prepositional phrase.

> They drove *around* the city to see the sights.
>
> When Jimin saw her parents coming, she ran *to* them.
>
> The horse jumped *over* the fence.
>
> Jayesh put his toys *in* the closet and went out to play *on* the swings.
>
> Lucia enjoyed herself *during* the dance.
>
> The team had a pizza party *after* the game.

For a list of prepositions, see "Common Prepositions" on page 139.

prepositional phrase

See "phrase" on page 98.

present participle

See "participle" on page 91.

present perfect tense

See "perfect tenses" on page 93.

progressive tenses

The progressive tenses are used to communicate about some action or state of being which is being continued.

There are three progressive tenses: present progressive, past progressive and future progressive.

1. Present progressive

Shows an action or state of being that is continuing in the present. It is formed with a verb phrase using *am, is* or *are* + the present participle.

Use the present progressive tense to talk about things or changes that are happening around the time of speaking but are not finished.

>We *are playing* the top team today.
>
>They *are being* very helpful.
>
>I *am speaking* at commencement this weekend.
>
>*Are* you *seeing* this movie for the first time?
>
>I can't understand why he *is* not *auditioning* for that role.

2. Past progressive

Shows an action or state of being which continued at some past time. It is formed with a verb phrase using *was* or *were* + the present participle.

>I *was cleaning* my dorm room last night.
>
>At this time last year, we *were living* at home in Canada.
>
>Joaquin yelled to Mia but she *was walking* the other way and didn't hear him.

Use the past progressive tense with the past tense when you want to communicate that something happened while something else was going on.

>My computer *broke* while we *were researching* the assignment for current events class.
>
>I *fell* off my horse while I *was taking* my riding lesson.

We *saw* you at the dance. You *didn't see* us because you *were dancing* and *talking* with friends the entire time.

3. Future progressive

Shows an action or state of being that will continue in the future. It uses *will* + *be* + present participle.

I *will be cooking* all day before the feast.

Minh *will be studying* all weekend.

Denise and Daniela *will be arranging* all the flowers for the event.

For more examples, see "Verb Tenses" on page 137.

pronoun

A pronoun is a word that takes the place of a noun. It is used to avoid repeating a noun over and over.

Without pronouns:
I've always loved my aunt. I used to visit my aunt every summer. My aunt often took us for long walks through the woods.

With pronouns:
I've always loved my aunt. I used to visit *her* every summer. *She* often took us for long walks through the woods.

There are six types of pronouns:

1. Personal pronouns

Used instead of the name of a person or sometimes a thing.

| *I* | *me* | *you* | *he* | *him* | *she* |
| *her* | *it* | *we* | *us* | *they* | *them* |

I went to see *him*.

Will *you* come with *us* to the concert?

They want to go to the party.

2. Possessive pronouns

Possessive pronouns are personal pronouns that show ownership.

mine   *yours*   *his*   *hers*
its   *ours*   *theirs*

Those keys are *mine*.
Don't take *hers*. Take *yours*.
Are any students' computers broken? *Theirs* are broken.

3. Reflexive pronouns

Reflexive means reflecting or turning back. Reflexive pronouns show that the subject of the sentence acts upon itself.

myself   *yourself*   *himself*   *herself*   *oneself*
itself   *ourselves*   *yourselves* *themselves*

I did it *myself*.
The bolt worked *itself* loose.
We fixed *ourselves* sandwiches for lunch.
The boys gave *themselves* a treat after the game.

Sometimes reflexive pronouns are used for emphasis.

I *myself* took those photographs.
After the loss, the team *itself* had a meeting without the coach.

4. Demonstrative pronouns

To demonstrate means to show. Demonstrative pronouns show or point out someone or something.

this   *that*   *these*   *those*

This is my new smart phone.
Give me *that*.

Those belong to Jane.

After looking over all the colors, *these* look best on you.

The word *this* and *that* (and their plurals *these* and *those*) can refer to many things. When writing, make sure your reader can easily tell what is being talked about.

Unclear: The store is being redesigned to increase efficiency and painted a different color. *This* irritates Tom.
(Is Tom irritated by the redesign or the new color or both?)

Clear: The store is being redesigned to increase efficiency and painted a different color. Tom is irritated by both of *these*.

Unclear: Tigers are terrifying, but lions don't bother me for some reason. *Those* have changed over the years.
(What's changed? Tigers? Lions? The person's feelings about them?)

Clear: Tigers are terrifying, but lions don't bother me for some reason. *Those* are my feelings today, but it used to be the other way around.

5. Interrogative pronouns

Interrogative means asking a question. Interrogative pronouns are used in place of a noun when asking a question.

> who   whom   which   whose   what

Who lives next door?

What is the name of your favorite book?

Whose is that?

6. Relative pronouns

Relative means related or connected in meaning. Relative pronouns are used to relate a group of words to something mentioned earlier in the sentence.

who *whom* *which* *what* *that*

The boy *who* won the race is fourteen years old.

The shirt, *which* is on sale, is green and white.

The gift was exactly *what* he'd hoped for.

He told me the same story *that* he told you yesterday.

7. Indefinite pronouns

Indefinite pronouns are used to talk or write about people or things without naming them exactly. The following are common ones:

all	*another*	*any*	*anybody*	*anyone*	*anything*
both	*each*	*either*	*everybody*	*everyone*	*everything*
few	*many*	*most*	*much*	*neither*	*no one*
nobody	*none*	*nothing*	*one*	*other*	*others*
several	*some*	*somebody*	*someone*	*something*	*such*

All are going to the game.

Few will take that test.

I will bring *something* that *everyone* will like.

Such is the way to show good manners.

Many of these same words can be used to modify a noun and when that occurs, they are modifiers not pronouns.

Pronoun	Modifier
Many will come soon.	*Many* people will come soon.
I have checked *most* for defects.	I have checked *most* computers for defects.

Here are some common indefinite pronouns that are singular and take a singular verb:

anybody   anyone   each   either   everybody   everyone
everything   neither   no one   nobody   nothing   somebody
someone   something

Nobody wants ice cream with the cake.

Someone is at the front door.

Here are some common indefinite pronouns that are plural and take a plural verb:

both   few   many   several

A *few* want ice cream with the cake.

Both are at the front door.

Here are some common indefinite pronouns that can be either singular or plural:

all   any   more
most   some   none

All of the children want ice cream with the cake.

All of the cake has been eaten.

For more examples, see pronoun usage #6 on page 109.

pronouns, jobs in a sentence

See "nouns and pronouns, jobs in a sentence" on page 89.

---

pronoun usage

1. Use a pronoun after the noun it replaces.

   Jenna always loved telling stories. *She* tells *them* now with photographs.

2. Make sure it's clear what noun is being replaced.

   Unclear: Alice and her mother walked into the store. *She* was carrying a package.

   Clear: Alice was carrying a package as *she* and her mother walked into the store.

   Unclear: The burglar left by the kitchen door and threw his gloves in the neighbor's trash. *That* was his big mistake.

   Clear: The burglar left by the kitchen door. Then he threw his gloves in the neighbor's trash and *that* was his big mistake.

3. Replace singular nouns with singular pronouns, plurals with plurals.

   Incorrect: Our neighbors want us to feed *her* dog while *she* is gone.

   Correct: Our neighbors want us to feed *their* dog while *they* are gone.

   Exception: When using a pronoun meaning "any person of any known or unknown gender," it is now acceptable to use *they* rather than *he*.

   Former usage: Everyone thinks *he* has a right to a free lunch.
   Current usage: Everyone thinks *they* have a right to a free lunch.

   or

Acceptable but awkward: *Everyone thinks he or she has a right to a free lunch.*

or

Making it plural instead: *People think they have a right to a free lunch.*

4. Use singular pronouns for countries and other collective identities.

   Incorrect: *France sent their troops to Russia. The government announced that they intended to raise taxes.*

   Correct: *France sent its troops to Russia. The government announced that it intended to raise taxes.*

5. Keep all pronouns in a compound subject or object in the correct case.

   Incorrect: *Joe and me aim to please.*
   Correct: *Joe and I aim to please.*

   Incorrect: *You and me went swimming yesterday.*
   Correct: *You and I went swimming yesterday*

   Incorrect: *Mrs. Hartley told Teddy and I to go outside.*
   Correct: *Mrs. Hartley told Teddy and me to go outside.*

   Incorrect: *You gave the cake to Joan and who?*
   Correct: *You gave the cake to Joan and whom?*

6. Pronouns and their verbs should agree in number.

This is often obvious:

He is on the varsity cheer team.
(subject and verb are both singular)

They are on the varsity cheer team.
(subject and verb are both plural)

It can get tricky when using an indefinite pronoun as a subject because some indefinite pronouns are singular, some are plural and some can be either, depending on the context. Yet, the verb of the sentence must agree with it in number.

Incorrect: *Everyone are* bringing food to the picnic.

Correct: *Everyone is* bringing food to the picnic.

Incorrect: Plan for extra people in case *several brings* their friends.

Correct: Plan for extra people in case *several bring* their friends.

Common indefinite pronouns that are singular:

anybody	*anyone*	*anything*	*everybody*	*everyone*
everything	*each*	*either*	*neither*	*no one*
nobody	*nothing*	*one*	*somebody*	*someone*
something				

Incorrect: *Anyone are* free to choose.

Correct: *Anyone is* free to choose.

Incorrect: John and his sister love performing in the school plays. *Neither are* auditioning this year, though.

Correct: John and his sister love performing in the school plays. *Neither is* auditioning this year, though.

Common indefinite pronouns that are plural:

both	*few*	*many*	*several*

Incorrect: *Both* of my parents *is* coming to the play.

Correct: *Both* of my parents *are* coming to the play.

Here are some indefinite pronouns that can be singular or plural, depending on the noun being referred to:

all   *any*   *more*   *most*

some   *none*

Incorrect: *All* of the girls *is* going to the prom.

Correct: *All* of the girls *are* going to the prom.

(*All* is plural because it refers to girls.)

Incorrect: *All* of my artwork *are* for sale.

Correct: *All* of my artwork *is* for sale.

(*All* is singular because it refers to artwork.)

run-on sentence

A run-on sentence consists of two or more complete sentences put together without an appropriate joining word or punctuation.

Example run-ons incorrectly connected by a comma:

Incorrect: I went home early, I ate some soup.

Correct: I went home early, and I ate some soup.

Incorrect: Jane was cheering loudly, her team had won the tournament.

Correct: Jane was cheering loudly. Her team had won the tournament!

Example run-ons incorrectly connected by an adverb:

Incorrect: The students lifted weights every day thus they developed greater upper body strength.

Correct: The students lifted weights every day. Thus, they developed greater upper body strength.

Example run-ons with no connecting word or punctuation at all:

Incorrect: The dog and the bunny chased each other around the yard they were great friends.

Correct: The dog and the bunny chased each other around the yard because they were great friends.

run-on sentence correction

There are several ways to correct a run-on sentence.

Run-on:

Jerry went to the store near his house, he bought some eggs.

1. The simplest correction is to separate the two independent clauses with a period, making each a separate sentence:

   Jerry went to the store near his house. He bought some eggs.

2. Sometimes it sounds better to join the clauses with a coordinating conjunction (*and, but, for, or, nor, yet, so*). Put a comma before the conjunction:

   Jerry went to the store near his house, *and* he bought some eggs.

   or

   Jerry went to the store near his house, *so* he bought some eggs.

3. If it makes sense, you can correct the run-on by adding a subordinating conjunction that makes one of the clauses dependent:

   Because Jerry went to the store near his house, he bought some eggs.

   or

   Since Jerry went to the store near his house, he bought some eggs.

4. Occasionally, it works to join the two clauses with a semicolon when their meaning is related:

Jerry went to the store near his house; he bought some eggs.

sentence

A group of words that has a subject and its verb, and that expresses a complete thought. It can be simple or complicated, short or long. It can have multiple subjects, verbs and descriptive phrases.

She likes fruit.

His mother likes to cook and eat all kinds of fruit.

His mother and father chop, bake, and eat fresh fruits and vegetables every weekend.

sentence fragment

A fragment is a small piece of something. A sentence fragment is a piece of a sentence written *as if it were* a sentence. It is *not* a complete sentence because it lacks a subject or its verb, or it does not express a complete thought.

Jenny and Josh

In the house

During the day

When the sun shines

After the party ends

simple subject

See "subject" on page 114.

---

subject

The subject of a sentence tells who or what is being, doing or having something in the sentence.

Josefina was my best friend in high school. (being)

My cat leapt off the top cabinet onto the table. (doing)

Ms. Brighton has a new delivery truck. (having)

A sentence always has a subject but sometimes it is implied, not stated.

(*You*) Be happy.

(*You*) Take your dog outside.

A simple subject is the noun or pronoun of the subject.

James, my good friend, is an excellent student.

A complete subject includes all the words that describe that noun or pronoun.

James, my good friend, is an excellent student.

Following are more examples. The simple subjects are in italics, and the complete subjects are underlined.

When there are no additional describing words, the simple subject and complete subject are the same, such as in the first three examples.

Joseph is learning how to swim.

She likes us most of the time.

Don't say that. (The subject *you* is implied.)

Many *people* find joy in dancing.

Now and then, <u>we *bakers*</u> like to experiment with wheat flour substitutes.

Screaming by at 200 miles per hour, <u>Kevin Harvick's number 4 *Mustang*</u> shot down the straightaway like a thunderbolt.

<u>The slanting *light* from the afternoon sun</u> warmed us on the grass.

<u>The dirty *trick* that he played on me</u> wasn't funny.

Notice that in the last two examples, a phrase (from the afternoon sun) and a clause (that he played on me) are part of the complete subject of the sentence.

Here are more examples showing a clause modifying the subject. Don't confuse the verb in the clause with the main verb in the sentence.

      subject   verb
<u>The *time* that I was talking about</u> was last week.

      subject   verb
<u>The *guy* I remember from school</u> pretended not to know me.

          subject   verb
<u>The lovely *music* that was playing in my ears</u> put me to sleep.

A sentence can have two or more connected subjects that have the same verb. This is a compound subject.

Sarah and *Julie* were roommates at school.

Happiness and *health* are the goal of many people.

He or *she* has permission to go on the trip.

Neither *Theo* nor his *brother* was eager to move to a new town.

subject of a sentence, finding

You can find the subject of a sentence with an action verb by asking, "Who or what is doing the action?"

You can find the subject of a sentence with a being verb by asking, "Who or what is being, existing or becoming?"

Jacques plays well.	Who or what plays well? *Jacques*
Discipline can be learned.	Who or what can be learned? *Discipline*
What did *the clever dog* do?	Who or what did something? *The clever dog*
When it rains, *the whole baseball team* practices in the gym.	Who or what practices in the gym? *The whole baseball team*
There are *flowers* all along the path.	Who or what are along the path? *Flowers*
Gabriella and Chloe are eighteen years old today.	Who is eighteen? *Gabriella and Chloe*

The subject in sentences expressing a command or request is *you* whether it appears or not.

(You) Take an umbrella. It's starting to rain.

(You) Please pick up my dry cleaning.

You must stay with the child.

Being able to find the subject of a sentence is especially useful when reading long, complex sentences.

When looking for the subject of a sentence, look in the independent clause. A sentence's subject will never be in a dependent clause or a phrase.

The following excerpts are taken from the book *Rifles for Watie* by Harold Keith.

> "Cut off from his rifle, which lay against a small hickory where they had skinned the beef, Jeff dived barefooted into a nearby thicket."

Where's the independent clause?
Jeff dived barefooted into a nearby thicket

Who dived?
Jeff. Jeff is the subject of this sentence.

> "When he had been on outpost duty there the day before, he had heard the voices of their pickets as they met across the river, and seen the faint illumination of their pipes through the shadowy cottonwoods and willows that lined the opposite shore, and smelled the fresh beef broiling over their campfires."

Where's the independent clause?
he had heard the voices of their pickets as they met across the river...

Who had heard and seen and smelled?
he. He is the subject of this sentence.

---

subject restatement

See "noun restatement" on page 88.

---

subject-verb agreement

A singular subject should have a singular verb and a plural subject should have a plural verb.

>Incorrect: The cat *eat* all her food.
>Correct: The cat *eats* all her food.
>
>Incorrect: The dogs *is* playing in the yard.
>Correct: The dogs *are* playing in the yard.

Ensuring the subject and verb agree can be tricky when a modifying phrase comes between the subject and verb.

Incorrect: A mob of angry men *are* unlikely to arrive at any sane course of action.

Correct: A mob of angry men *is* unlikely to arrive at any sane course of action.

(*Mob* is a singular subject so the sentence should have the singular verb *is*, despite the prepositional phrase with a plural object.)

Incorrect: The products of a competent person *demonstrates* quality and attention to detail.

Correct: The products of a competent person *demonstrate* quality and attention to detail.

Incorrect: A hive of bees *are* sometimes dangerous.

Correct: A hive of bees *is* sometimes dangerous.

subjunctive mood

See "mood (or mode) of verbs" on page 83.

subordinating conjunction

See "conjunction" on page 74.

T

tense

The form of a verb that shows when something happens or exists. Verbs change in form to show different times—past, present or future.

Present tense	Past tense	Future tense
The women *sing*.	The women *sang*.	The women *will sing*.
They *are* students.	They *were* students last year.	They *will be* students next year.

For more examples of all tenses, see "Verb Tenses" on page 137.

transition

A word or group of words that helps connect sentences or paragraphs together, such as *thus, however, for this reason,* or *because of this.*

transitive verb

See "verb, transitive and intransitive" on page 121.

verb

A word that communicates action or being. It is the verb of a sentence that tells what is happening or existing.

This gives us two types of verbs: action verbs and being verbs.

Examples of sentences with action verbs:

> Lily *ran* and *jumped* into her mother's arms.
>
> I *wish* that she had called.
>
> Truthfully, the time *has passed* much more quickly than I thought.
>
> Slowly but surely, we *are getting* this ditch dug.
>
> *Have* you *forgotten* how to get there?

Examples of sentences with being verbs:

> He *was* a veterinarian for twenty years.
>
> Apples *are* delicious.
>
> The old woman on Parker Street only *seems* to be unfriendly.
>
> She *was*n't the person I was talking about.
>
> I've suddenly *become* incapable of solving these problems.

Some verbs can be action verbs or being verbs depending on how they're used.

> That dog *smells* me from a mile away. (action)
> That flower *smells* wonderful. (being)
>
> Please *taste* my freshly baked apple pie. (action)
> It *tastes* delicious! (being)

Every sentence or question must have at least one verb.

> The puppy *ran* around the room.
>
> The children *read* books and *wrote* in their journals for three hours.
>
> What *happened*?
>
> Who *will be visiting* tomorrow?

verb of a sentence, finding

To find the verb of a sentence, look in the independent clause for the word telling what action or state of being the sentence is communicating about.

> The team played their best game last week.
> **What did the team do? The team *played***
>
> Jimmy rides his bicycle everywhere that he needs to go.
> **What does Jimmy do? Jimmy *rides***
>
> Spring is early this year.
> **What about spring? Spring *is***
>
> After studying and working for eight years, Jessica has become a doctor.
> **What about Jessica? She *has become***

verb, transitive and intransitive

Transitive means "goes across."

transitive verb

A transitive verb is a verb where the action goes across to the direct object.

> Joseph *broke* the window.
> (The action goes across. *Window* is the direct object.)

The bird *sang* a beautiful song.
(The action goes across. *Song* is the direct object.)

She *won* the contest.
(The action goes across. *Contest* is the direct object.)

intransitive verb

In- means "not." An intransitive verb is a verb where the action does not go across. It has no direct object.

Here are examples of sentences with intransitive verbs:

The carpenter *worked* long and hard.
(This sentence has no direct object.)

Rebecca *laughed* loudly.
(This sentence has no direct object.)

The cow *jumped* over the fence.
(This sentence has no direct object. *Over the fence* is a prepositional phrase describing where the cow jumped.)

Many verbs can be transitive or intransitive depending on how they're used:

She often *forgets* my name. **Transitive.**

She often *forgets*. **Intransitive.**

Teresa *swung* and *missed*. **Both verbs are intransitive.**

Teresa *swung* the bat and *missed* the ball. **Both verbs are transitive.**

He *writes* thoughtfully and beautifully. **Intransitive.**

He *writes* articles for magazines. **Transitive.**

An intransitive verb can communicate an action, ownership or result but it does not happen to a direct object.

It's useful to know the difference between transitive and intransitive verbs when looking up words in the dictionary. Most dictionaries tell whether a definition of a verb is transitive or intransitive so you can understand how to use the word correctly.

The way dictionaries label transitive and intransitive verbs varies. Here are the most common:

transitive	intransitive
trans.	*intrans.*
v.t. (for *verb transitive*)	*v.i.* (for *verb intransitive*)
t.	*i.*
(with object)	*(without object)*

All being verbs are intransitive.

> I *am* a fireman.
>
> The truck *was* bright red.
>
> Those cookies *smell* good.
>
> She *became* a doctor.
>
> She has to *be* the nicest person I've ever met.

APPENDIX

Grammar at a Glance

NOUNS

TYPES OF NOUNS

common noun

A word that names a person, place, thing, or idea.

> *person, holiday, state, country, freedom*

> That person is from my favorite *country*.

proper noun

A word that names a specific person, place, thing, or idea; it is always capitalized.

> *Elizabeth Jones, Rami Singh, New Year's Day, Texas, India, Golden Gate Bridge*

> *Rami* celebrated *New Year's Day* in *Texas* this year.

collective noun

A word that names a group of persons, places, things, or ideas.

> **singular:** *family, team, flock*

>> *My family meets in Aspen every year for a ski vacation.*

> **plural:** *families, teams, flocks*

>> *Our families meet in Aspen every year for a ski vacation.*

JOBS THAT NOUNS (AND PRONOUNS) DO IN SENTENCES

subject
The noun that is having, being, or doing something in a sentence.

> The *team* has an election for their new captain every year.
>
> Her *writing* improved with practice.
>
> *Emile* is an extraordinary piano player.

direct object
The noun that the action of the verb is directed to.

> The teacher gave *awards* to students for excellent work.
>
> Ken caught the *ball* and saved the goal.

indirect object
The noun that tells who or what the action of the verb is being done to.

> The father taught his *daughter* a new trick.
>
> Suzie gave the *garden* a good watering.

object of a preposition
The noun that ends a prepositional phrase.

> Kareem ran down the *hill*.
>
> The train went through the beautiful *countryside* of *Italy*.

noun restatement
A second noun that restates a previous noun in that sentence.

> We are going to have lunch with my brother, *Billy*.
>
> Our best soccer players are *Javier* and *Colin*.

Pronouns can do all the jobs that nouns do.

PRONOUNS

TYPES OF PRONOUNS

1. personal pronouns

I	me	you	he	him	she
her	it	we	us	they	them

Possessive pronouns

mine	yours	his	hers
its	ours	theirs	

2. reflexive pronouns

myself	yourself	himself	herself	oneself
itself	ourselves	yourselves	themselves	

3. demonstrative pronouns

this	that	those	these

That is exactly what I said.

Who gave you *this*?

I've never seen *those* before.

4. interrogative pronouns (pronouns used to ask a question.)

who	whom	which	whose	what

Which is the tiger you were talking about?

Who gave you this?

To *whom* was the letter addressed?

5. relative pronouns

(Pronouns that relate a phrase or clause to a previous noun, noun phrase or noun clause.)

who *whom* *which* *what* *that*

The girl *who* won the science fair built a time machine.

The gift was exactly *what* he had hoped for.

This couldn't be the answer, *which* is what I told you yesterday.

6. indefinite pronouns

(Pronouns used to talk about people or things without naming them exactly.)

These are some of the common indefinite pronouns.

all	*another*	*any*	*anybody*	*anyone*	*anything*
both	*each*	*either*	*everybody*	*everyone*	*everything*
few	*many*	*most*	*much*	*neither*	*no one*
nobody	*none*	*nothing*	*one*	*other*	*others*
several	*some*	*somebody*	*someone*	*something*	*such*

Few will take that test.

Somebody took the book off the shelf.

Such is the way to show your appreciation.

CASES OF PRONOUNS

Most pronouns have different forms for each case. Here are all the forms of pronouns for all three cases.

(used for subjects)	(used for objects)	(used for ownership)
<u>nominative case</u>	<u>objective case</u>	<u>possessive case</u>
I	*me*	*mine*
you	*you*	*yours*
he	*him*	*his*
she	*her*	*hers*
it	*it*	*its*
we	*us*	*ours*
they	*them*	*theirs*
who	*whom*	*whose*

VERBS

TYPES OF VERBS

action verbs

examples:

run, play, eat, sing, sleep, quit, wonder, try, imagine

being verbs

examples:

be, is, am, are, was, were, seem, become

Action verbs can be transitive (with a direct object) or intransitive (without a direct object) depending on their use in a sentence.

Transitive action verbs:

The girls *sing* that song very well.

We *play* professional basketball.

Intransitive action verbs:

The girls *sing* very well.

We *play* for the Los Angeles Lakers.

Being verbs are always intransitive.

Anna *is* a good volleyball player.

Alejandro *became* a doctor last year.

(*Player* and *doctor* are not direct objects, they are noun restatements.)

FORMS OF VERBS

There are four basic forms for any verb. To demonstrate, here are the four verb forms for *work*:

1. **infinitive**   *(to) work*

   Work is the basic form of the verb, called the infinitive (or *base* or *root* form). The infinitive expresses the action or state of being, without limiting it to a tense or person.

   It can also be written *to work*. Here *to* has no meaning, but just shows the verb is in the infinitive form.

   Jonathan wanted to work all summer.

2. **present participle**   *working*

   A present participle is always formed by adding *-ing* to the infinitive.

   She is working tonight.

   He was working all day.

   Jennifer will be working there tomorrow.

3. **past**   *worked*

   Most often, the past tense is formed by adding *-d* or *-ed* to the infinitive.

   William worked for forty hours.

   With irregular verbs, such as *have* or *think*, the past form varies.

   We had a good time yesterday.

   He thought about his friend.

4. **past participle**   *(have) worked*

The past participle is used with a form of *have* to make tenses that communicate completed actions.

She has worked in the library all morning.

Sally had worked there for thirty years.

By January, Jim will have worked here for one year.

SOME REGULAR VERBS

Infinitive	Present Participle	Past	Past Participle
(to) stay	staying	stayed	(have) stayed
(to) work	working	worked	(have) worked
(to) talk	talking	talked	(have) talked
(to) use	using	used	(have) used

SOME COMMON IRREGULAR VERBS

Irregular verbs do not form the past and past participle by adding *-d* or *–ed*.

Infinitive	Present Participle	Past	Past Participle
(to) be	being	was, were	(have) been
(to) begin	beginning	began	(have) begun
(to) bring	bringing	brought	(have) brought
(to) come	coming	came	(have) come
(to) dive	diving	dove or dived	(have) dived
(to) do	doing	did	(have) done
(to) drink	drinking	drank	(have) drunk

Infinitive	Present Participle	Past	Past Participle
(to) eat	eating	ate	(have) eaten
(to) have	having	had	(have) had
(to) lay	laying	laid	(have) laid
(to) lead	leading	led	(have) led
(to) lie	lying	lay	(have) lain
(to) know	knowing	knew	(have) known
(to) pay	paying	paid	(have) paid
(to) run	running	ran	(have) run
(to) say	saying	said	(have) said
(to) see	seeing	saw	(have) seen
(to) sing	singing	sang	(have) sung
(to) sit	sitting	sat	(have) sat
(to) take	taking	took	(have) taken
(to) throw	throwing	threw	(have) thrown
(to) write	writing	wrote	(have) written

Dictionary entries for verbs give the infinitive, or base, form.

For irregular verbs, many dictionaries will follow the entry with the past and past participle forms. They do not show the past and past participle forms for regular verbs, which are formed by simply adding -d or –ed.

VERB TENSES

There are six basic tenses:

present	present perfect
past	past perfect
future	future perfect

present tense

The women *laugh*.

They *are* students this year.

past tense

The women *laughed*.

They *were* students last year.

future tense

The women *will laugh*.

They *will be* students next year.

The perfect tenses use a form of *have* plus the past participle to show that an action or state of being has been completed.

present perfect

The women *have laughed*.

They *have been* students this year.

past perfect

The women *had laughed*.

They *had been* students before this year.

future perfect

The women *will have laughed*.

They *will have been* students by next week.

Each of the six basic tenses has a **progressive tense** that communicates the idea of an action or state of being continuing.

Examples of the six basic tenses with progressive tenses.

Present	She *sings* today.
Past	He *sang* yesterday.
Future	They *will sing* tomorrow.
Present Progressive	She *is singing* today.
Past Progressive	He *was singing* yesterday.
Future Progressive	They *will be singing* tomorrow.
Present Perfect	She *has sung* already today.
Past Perfect	He *had sung* two hours yesterday before noon.
Future Perfect	On Friday, they *will have sung* for seven days straight.
Present Perfect Progressive	She *has been singing* all week.
Past Perfect Progressive	He *had been singing* for two hours when I called him.
Future Perfect Progressive	By next year, they *will have been singing* there for five years.

PREPOSITIONS

COMMON PREPOSITIONS

about	*behind*	*except*	*out*	*until*
above	*below*	*for*	*over*	*up*
across	*beneath*	*from*	*past*	*upon*
after	*beside*	*in*	*since*	*with*
along	*between*	*into*	*through*	*within*
among	*beyond*	*near*	*to*	*without*
around	*by*	*of*	*toward*	
at	*down*	*off*	*under*	
before	*during*	*on*	*underneath*	

They drove *around* the city to see the sights.

When Jimin saw her parents coming, she ran *to them*.

The horse jumped *over the fence*.

Jayesh put his toys in the closet and went out to play *on the swings*.

Lucia enjoyed herself *during the dance*.

They enjoyed jumping *off* the bridge *into* the river.

The rocket launched *into* space *at* an alarming speed *with* a terrific noise.

Frank said to walk *through* the field, *beneath* the highway, and *toward* the tallest building *on* the horizon *until* noon.

CONJUNCTIONS

COORDINATING CONJUNCTIONS

Conjunctions that join similar words, phrases, or clauses.

for	The children were tired, *for* the day had been long.
and	They ate at the Thai restaurant, *and* then they went to that new movie.
nor	She won't go to that movie, *nor* will she see any horror movie.
but	Carlie wanted to learn both languages, *but* she chose Japanese.
or	They served coffee, tea, *or* hot cider at the Fall Festival.
yet	Graham was cold, *yet* he didn't want to go inside.
so	Ahmed was hungry, *so* he made himself some breakfast.

FANBOYS, made from the first letter of each, can help you remember the seven main coordinating conjunctions.

CORRELATIVE CONJUNCTIONS

Pairs of words that join equal elements in a sentence.

either...or	She is going to Indonesia to teach *either* English *or* French.
neither...nor	*Neither* he *nor* I could solve the riddle.
both...and	My favorite teacher was *both* a mentor *and* a friend.
not only...but also	He studied *not only* biology *but also* chemistry last year.
whether...or	I have to decide *whether* to play volleyball *or* soccer.

SUBORDINATING CONJUNCTIONS

Words that start an adverb clause and join it to the independent clause of a sentence.

These words are commonly used as this type of conjunction:

after	*although*	*as*
as if	*as though*	*as long as*
because	*before*	*if*
in order that	*since*	*so that*
than	*though*	*unless*
until	*when*	*whenever*
where	*wherever*	*while*

Subordinating conjunctions begin dependent clauses that act as adverbs by modifying the main verb.

Since she wanted that job, Mia prepared thoroughly for the job interview.

Rio went to sleep early *because* he was going to run a marathon the next day.

Whenever you talk about Robert, I start laughing.

I'm leaving for Germany *so that* I can meet with the company president.

After she tried out for choir, she knew she was going to enjoy it.

PHRASES

prepositional phrase

A group of words that starts with a preposition and ends with a noun or pronoun.

> They enjoyed their drive *through the countryside.*
> The children loved playing *at the beach.*
> They swam *in the ocean.*

adjective phrase

A prepositional phrase that modifies a noun or pronoun.

> Students *from our school* read many books each year.
> The books *on our reading lists* vary greatly.
> Most students read my favorite book *about Michelangelo.*

adverb phrase

A phrase that modifies a verb or modifier in a sentence.

> The choir practices many months *before every concert.*
> She plays piano *for the winter concerts.*
> The piano sounds *absolutely perfect.*

noun phrase

A phrase acting as a noun and containing an *–ing* verb.

> *Finding the ideal career* is the goal of many college students.
> He took *painting lessons* in art school.
> *Scuba diving safely* is necessary for a marine biologist.

infinitive phrase

A phrase that starts with *to* and ends with a verb.

> She learned *to swim* when she was 2 years old.
>
> He finds it easy *to write* when he knows the subject well.
>
> When do you plan *to send* your email?

CLAUSES

independent clause

Expresses a complete thought with a subject and its verb

My mother is planning a trip to Asia.

Our parents traveled through Western Europe into Poland.

dependent clause

Does not express a complete thought but has a subject and its verb

so that we could study

since it was raining

when I studied in London

TYPES OF DEPENDENT CLAUSES

adjective clause

A dependent clause that modifies a noun or pronoun.

My sister, who is a chemistry major, helps me with my homework.

Yesterday, I scored a goal that I thought was impossible.

Was she the one who won the contest?

adverb clause

A dependent clause that modifies a verb or another modifier.

We went to the library so that we could study.

Since it was raining, we didn't go on a hike.

I earned a degree in finance when I studied in London.

noun clause

A dependent clause that acts as a noun in a sentence.

What the newspaper reported was only part of the story.

The teacher knew *that her students invented something extraordinary.*

The instructor gave *whoever needed them* materials for the project.

INDEX

A

adjective incorrectly used as adverb, 59
  good/well, 60

apostrophe
  not used for possessive pronouns, 26

article
  usage, 64

B

brackets
  acting or stage directions, 34
  errors or additional data in quotation, 34
  in text already within parentheses, 34
  uses, 34

C

capitalization
  main words of titles, 48

case
  nouns, 67
  pronouns, 65

clause
  adjective, 70
  adverb, 70
  chart, 145
  dependent, 69
  independent, 69
  nonrestrictive, 72
  noun, 71
  restrictive, 71

colloquial language, 72

colon
  means "note what follows", 27

comma
  approaches, 9
  introductory adverb clause, 13
  locations, 13
  nonrestrictive clause or phrase, 18
  not between preposition and its object, 22
  rules, 10
    after a long introductory prepositional phrase that modifies, 15
    after an introductory adverb clause, 13

after an introductory participle phrase, 14
after a short introductory modifier, 15
after most introductory conjunctions and adverbs, 16
around a person or thing being addressed, 11
at both ends of a nonrestrictive element in mid-sentence, 19
between a preposition and its object, 22
between a subject and its verb, 21
between a verb and direct object, 22
between independent clauses, 17
between items connected by and[italic] or or[italic], 22
between multiple modifiers, 11
for clarity, 23
items in a list or series, 10
with a nonrestrictive clause or phrase, 18
with a restrictive phrase or clause, 20
without a specific rule, 23
write dates and locations, 12
writing an exact quotation, 11

compound modifier, 73

conjunction, 74
  chart, 140

dash
  general use, 41

direct object, 77

ellipsis
  use, 45

end marks
  definition, 5

exclamation point
  use, 7

grammar
  definition, 57
  use, 58

H

helping verb
  also auxiliary, 79

hyphen
  compound modifier after noun, 43

I

indirect object, 80

italics
emphasis, 54

Its/it's, correct use, 26

J

jobs that nouns and pronouns do in sentences
chart, 129

N

no comma
adverb clause at end of sentence, 14
before conjunction when two verbs share same subject, 17
between a verb and direct object, 22
between items connected by and, or, 22
between preposition and its object, 22
month and year only, 13

noun
cases, 67
chart, 128
collective, 87
definition, 86
proper, 88

noun restatement
definition, 88
subject restatement, 88

nouns and pronouns
jobs in a sentence, 89

P

parallel structure
usage, 90

parentheses
comment not vital to meaning of sentence, 31
dates, 32
documentation, 31
use, 31

participle
usage, 92

perfect progressive tenses
future perfect progressive, 96
past perfect progressive, 95
present perfect progressive, 95

perfect tenses
future perfect, 94
past perfect, 94
use, 93

period
after abbreviation, 5
end of every statement, 5
list using numbers or letters, 6

person
first, 96
second, 97

third, 97
third person pronoun use, 98

phrase
adjective, 98
adverb, 98
chart, 143
definition, 98
nonrestrictive, 100
noun, 99
participle, 99
prepositional, 99
restrictive, 100

preposition
chart, 139
definition, 101
object, 89

progressive tenses
future progressive, 103
past progressive, 102
present progressive, 102
use, 102

pronoun
chart, 130
chart of cases, 132
definition, 103
indefinite pronoun use, 106
nominative case, 66
objective case, 66
possessive case, 67

pronoun usage
agreement, 108, 109

punctuation
with parentheses, 32
with quotation marks, 36

question mark
can show uncertainty, 6
when asking a question, 6

quotation
direct, 35
not for indirect, 35

quotation marks
punctuation with, 36
single, 38
used in text, 38

run-on sentence
correction, 112
definition, 111

semicolon
not followed by fragment, 29

slash, 45

subject of a sentence
complete subject, 114
compound subject, 115
definition, 114
finding, 116
implied (understood), 114
simple subject, 114

subject restatement
definition, 88

T

tense
chart, 137
definition, 119
progressive, 102

titles
essays, reports, research papers, 48

U

underlines, 53, 54

V

verb
action, 120
being, 120
being verbs are intransitive, 123
chart, 133
chart of irregular verbs, 135
chart of verb forms, 134
definition, 120
finding, 121
helping, 79
infinitive form, 81
intransitive, 122
mood (or mode), 83
transitive, 121